KIDS GET STRESSED TOO

understanding what's going on & how to help

Erin Whelan

KIDS GET STRESSED TOO

understanding what's going on & how to help

Eileen McGrath, Ph.D.

ThomasMore®
– An RCL Company –
Allen, Texas

Send all inquiries to:

Thomas More
An RCL Company
200 East Bethany Drive
Allen, Texas 75002-3804

BOOKSTORES:
    Call Bookworld Companies 888-444-2524 or fax 941-753-9396
PARISHES AND SCHOOLS:
    Thomas More Publishing 800-822-6701 or fax 800-688-8356
INTERNATIONAL:
    Fax Thomas More Publishing 972-264-3719

Visit our website at www.rclweb.com

Printed in the United States of America

Library of Congress Card Number 99-75187

ISBN 0–88347–406–0

1 2 3 4 5   03 02 01 00 99

TABLE OF CONTENTS

INTRODUCTION   7

1 ☆ THE WORLD: FRIEND OR FOE?   11

2 ☆ STRESS: DO WE ELIMINATE IT
    OR TEACH KIDS HOW TO HANDLE IT?   21

3 ☆ KIDS *ON TRACK* AND KIDS *OFF TRACK*   45

4 ☆ HELPING CHILDREN HANDLE LOSS   69

5 ☆ STRESS AT SCHOOL   93

6 ☆ CHALLENGES FROM SOCIETY   103

7 ☆ WHAT CAN PARENTS AND TEACHERS DO?   115

8 ☆ BLOOM AND GROW TO THE FULLEST   127

Introduction

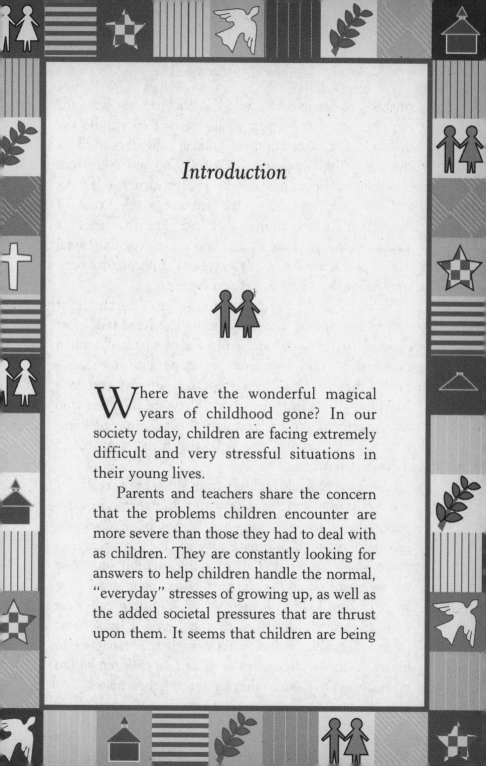

Where have the wonderful magical years of childhood gone? In our society today, children are facing extremely difficult and very stressful situations in their young lives.

Parents and teachers share the concern that the problems children encounter are more severe than those they had to deal with as children. They are constantly looking for answers to help children handle the normal, "everyday" stresses of growing up, as well as the added societal pressures that are thrust upon them. It seems that children are being pushed too far and too fast, and they do not have the developmental or coping skills needed to handle the pressure. For some children, gone are the days of "kick the can," "hide-and-seek," and playing sports for fun. Children are being pushed into independence, self-care, self-reliance, and, in some instances, the role of "caregiver" for a younger sibling. The incidence of stress-related physical illness and mental or emotional health problems, for adults as well as children, has risen tremendously over the past two decades.

Is it all "doom and gloom" in the life of the children? No, of course not! Some researchers believe that most children are resilient and will be able to handle much of the stress they encounter and cope with it successfully. These are the kids who feel support and love from the adults in their world. They are the ones who have been taught or, through the example of care-givers, have "caught" the skills they need to adjust to their environment.

We cannot shield children from stress or the reality of a sometimes chaotic, unsafe world, but there are ways parents and teachers can help. This book does not pretend to have the ultimate answers. It is an attempt to share some useful and helpful information on stress management for adults and kids, and to suggest positive ways to help kids with their world. Children can learn and develop the coping skills they need. I hope these pages will enable you, the parent, teacher, or caregiver, to better understand the stresses placed on children and to be a support to them as they experience their lives.

Today's society encourages and emphasizes the important role of family. School districts, town meetings, and television stations are sponsoring programs in various states to support families and allow parents to vent their concerns about their kids. They are able to ask their questions and receive guidance and parenting tips from other parents and experts in the area of family life. It is in the family where the foundation is laid and life education begins. Family is the first school, the first Church, where parents are the first teachers, imparting by word and example their faith, family values, and the morals that they believe and practice. Our children are constantly watching and absorbing our teachings and behavior. Most parents agree that there is no one set formula or an absolute guarantee of success. We can only try to be the best support and the best parents that we can. We can respect and revere each child as an individual, with a unique personality, special gifts, and certain limitations. It will be said many times throughout this book that there are no perfect parents and no perfect kids. Each of us may believe that we or our children are the exception to this rule. Hopefully, we will expect the best and accept the best that our child can do and be. However, we should always be aware that perfection is a goal, although unattainable here on this planet because we are all human. Young adults who feel a certain amount of security, success, and self-confidence attribute their well-being to parents who loved them and were really there for them as they grew up. We can be instruments of healing, forming strong families, enabling children to continue to grow in their faith, to have hope and trust in God, and to know that they are cherished, cared for, and loved simply because of who they are.

The stories in this book are true. Some are composites of actual events; the names of all the children are fictitious to protect their anonymity. Furthermore, we realize that some people may feel offended by the use of the word "kids." It is purposely used in this book to try to create an atmosphere of love, warmth, familiarity, and informality. No offense is intended.

Eileen McGrath, Ph.D.

–1–

THE WORLD: FRIEND OR FOE?

Accepting Life On Life's Terms

How can we help the kids to better understand their world and teach them the tools
they need to have a better life? One area that
comes to mind is the idea of control. What is
it? Who has it? How do we get it? Young
children need to believe that the adults in
their lives are in control. This provides kids
with a sense of security and the feeling that
they will get the care they need and will be
safe. They eventually see that their parents
and teachers are not necessarily in control
of everything. This message is learned

repeatedly whenever there is a trauma or tragic event. After such an incident, kids need to talk about it, express their fear and concern, and be encouraged to pick themselves up and continue moving forward. This is one of life's realities: that tragedy, traumas, and natural disasters occur. Rather than be paralyzed by fear, kids need the repeated assurance that each day must be faced with hope, that they must trust that they are safe, so they can get on with the process of living. To help lessen or eliminate apprehension and fear, adults may encourage the kids to mentally repeat a prayer or positive affirmation such as "I am safe. God's love surrounds me."

Instead of dashing their hopes and dreams, one of the first lessons to teach children may be that there are things over which we have no control. The only control we do have, theoretically, is over ourselves, the choices we make, and how we respond to things that happen to us. We are born into a certain family, a certain set of circumstances. We have an individual genetic makeup, such as our DNA, eye color, and fingerprints, unique to each person. We all have certain gifts that we may develop as we grow. We all have definite limitations. However, we are each lovable and capable of certain things. This is not a contest nor should it be a comparison. Each of us is unique and special in all the universe. There is not another person with our individual makeup. Each person is in charge, in control, of his/her choices. Children need to learn inner control to develop responsible and appropriate behavior. They also need to learn that with each choice there is a definite consequence. Developing a healthy self-esteem can have a positive effect on kids' choices, their behavior, and their sense of control.

Self-Esteem

Many of us have been taught that we are made in the image and likeness of God, and God doesn't make junk. We need to believe this, because it is true. To acquire a healthy self-esteem is a lifelong journey, a path where we learn to love and accept ourselves, to believe in and strive for our true potential. A healthy self-esteem is an essential key to life. It is not about being conceited or obnoxious or "tooting your own horn." These are the characteristics of someone with a very low self-esteem. If we can begin to know and love ourselves and recognize our gifts, we will not have to put somebody else down. What we believe about ourselves will enhance life and enable us to be fortified and ready to handle the experiences we choose and those that life presents. Our belief about ourselves has been affected by messages and attitudes received from others: parents, relatives, friends, peers, teachers, and even ourselves. If these messages are negative or real "put-downs," we begin to believe them. These become the foundation for how we look at and believe in ourselves. Some of these bad, hurtful messages are carried within our minds and believed into adulthood.

☆ ☆ ☆

A five-year-old girl was told repeatedly that she was unlovable. She heard this message so many times from her father that she lived in fear, and doubted that she could ever have a love relationship since she believed she truly was unlovable. When she was thirty years old, she did meet someone, fall in love, marry, and have two children. But if anything went wrong, or if she and her husband disagreed, that horrible feeling and belief of being unlovable welled up within her; she lived in constant fear that she would be abandoned. These feelings had a negative effect on her relationship. Her husband wearied of constantly trying to calm her fears and reassure her that she was loved. She sought counseling when she was in her forties. With hard work she gradually increased her self-esteem and canceled the negative message that had haunted her for many years. She continues to work on her self-esteem as she strives to eliminate her fear of abandonment.

This little girl is just one of many kids who have received devastating messages. When we listen to our inner voice, what message comes through? Do we believe it and repeat it many times to ourselves? Does this message build us up? Does it make us feel good so we can love and approve of ourselves? Does it help us attain a healthy relationship in our lives? Or does it tear us down and create doubt and feelings of self-loathing? How long will we continue to hold onto and believe the negative message we heard from someone as children? Perhaps we were told we were not good enough, or we could never do anything right. These statements were possibly made in anger or by someone with their own very low opinion of themselves. We realize now, as adults, that these remarks are not true. At that early age, we did not have the skills or the maturity to shake it off or prevent it from hurting us. It was probably almost impossible for us to process that hurt and realize it was a lie, definitely not to be believed. We *are* lovable, we *can* do things right, and we *are* good enough. God loves us, knows how hard we try to be the best person we can be, and God appreciates every single effort we make to be that good person. We are loved and cherished by God. Can we pass that message on to the kids whose lives we touch? We can teach them the skills they need to develop a good self-esteem and teach them how to cancel those negative messages they already have in their heads. We can also consciously refrain from giving kids those hurtful and debilitating negative messages.

Our self-esteem affects our self-confidence and our self-worth. Our esteem affects our attitude toward control and how much of it we will give away to others and under what circumstances.

Thirteen-year-old Jamie had a fifteen-year-old boyfriend who treated her terribly. He constantly put her down, punched her when he was upset by things she said, and called her negative and demeaning names. He wanted her to talk and act in a certain way, the way he thought she should. Jamie was afraid of losing him, fearing she wouldn't have a boyfriend, so she continued to stay in this abusive relationship.

☆ ☆ ☆

15

If we find ourselves in a relationship that is not life-giving, we must love ourselves enough to make a choice, and either get help or get out of the relationship.

Without self-respect, life will be so much harder than it needs to be. Our self-esteem affects us, either in a positive or negative way, at home, in school, in our relationships, at work, at play, and in every area of our lives. Parents, teachers, and any other well-meaning adults who interact with children must recognize their responsibility to be a role model and to enable kids to develop a healthy self-esteem. The sooner we encourage and support kids to believe in themselves and their gifts, the happier and healthier they will be. It will also help them to better understand the concept of control.

Courtney was born with a severe hearing impairment. She was the youngest of seven, and all her life her parents and siblings treated her as normally as possible. They encouraged her, listened to her, and basically told her she could do and be whatever she chose. She was mainstreamed all through school, was the president of her class, and was an "A" student. She had a wonderful outgoing, perky personality, and at the beginning of each school year, on orientation day, she was the one who not only met every classmate but also knew all their names. It was not until she was in college that she realized she was "different." She had so adjusted to her hearing loss, she was able to lip-read and communicate with others. The saddest and hardest struggle for

16

her was to realize she didn't have many close friends. This was probably because her speech was somewhat difficult to understand, and kids tended to shy away from her. She did have two close girlfriends who stuck by her; they are all still friends today. She has overcome these obstacles, graduated with honors from college, and is now a teacher in special education classes where the kids love her. She even received the Teacher of the Year award. Courtney is now in a loving relationship, planning to marry soon. Because of the love, support, and encouragement of her family and her own self-confidence, she has blossomed into a very mature, successful, well-adjusted, loving adult.

Another hard life lesson to be learned by adults and taught to kids is to accept life on life's terms. This does not mean that we are passive observers or victims or that we should adopt the stance of "oh well, poor me, there is nothing I can do about anything." We should work toward an attitude of living, which means to acknowledge and try to accept that there are certain things that we cannot change. All our arguing, fighting, wishing, and resistance will not make life change. Developing an attitude of living is to do the best we can with whatever we have. Making choices for today, for this moment, will enable us to be the best we can be.

There are many kids who have been dealt some pretty hard circumstances, some with partial disabilities, some paralyzed for life due to an accident or an act of violence. There are kids living with cancer or some other life-threatening or genetic disease, some living in poverty, and others living in pain, suffering, and abuse. Some of these kids, through their resilience and powerful spirit, have managed to deal with, and even overcome, these tremendous difficulties to continue to live a quality life. We have all heard about perceiving the glass as being half empty or half full. We can look at an experience as a major problem or a major challenge. Most of these kids have worked hard at acknowledging their conditions. Some are resigned to them and others have truly attained acceptance of their circumstances. But these kids must face additional distress over and above their physical reality. They must face that they are not usually accepted by their peers. They are perceived as "different"; because their peers do not want to be classified or labeled in any way that is different too, they are afraid or embarrassed to be with them.

This is a complex issue that needs to be addressed in "healthy kids." It is hard enough for kids to deal with their limitations without the added upheaval that comes from being isolated or avoided by their peers. The reality of life is that we are all different. Kids need to learn that "different" does not have to mean odd, strange, or weird. It is usually only a certain behavior that one chooses to act out which could elicit such a label. Different is good; it is a positive. This is exactly the point—that labels disable us and others. Labels are judgments and criticisms that lead to prejudice and a lack of tolerance or acceptance of each person as an individual. This is where respect for others and feelings of empathy need to be developed, modeled by adults, and encouraged in kids. Kids learn, incorporate, and perpetuate the values and morals they experience in their first school of life, the home and family. If they have to live with constant criticism or prejudice, they will learn to condemn and criticize and will have a zero tolerance for others.

Kids born with disabilities or kids with other disabling diseases do not deserve to be punished through isolation or ridicule by other kids. They didn't ask for their condition. These are the really true, brave little heroes who are constantly dealing with life on life's terms. Even a child with the most severe disability or one with the most grotesque features deserves care, respect, and unconditional love. That child is unique and special, and he/she brings the gift of love to his/her family. Education and awareness are needed in this area so children can learn to be more sensitive to others and to appreciate the fact that we all have our own gifts, talents, and limitations. Attitude does play a major role in facing any challenge.

Some kids will choose life, love, hard work, and good fun, while others will give up, wallow in self-pity, or resort to some other self-destructive behavior, such as using alcohol or drugs to mask their pain. What is it in the human spirit that makes one kid choose one way over the other? Many researchers believe that it is the parental attitude, their beliefs, their love, support, and encouragement that most affects the child's outlook on different life situations. Attitude adjustments begin in the adults and then filter down to the kids.

Another chapter of life's lessons that kids need to understand is that we constantly grow and change. We change and grow in the womb, in birth, and with each additional day and year of life. We have changed even since beginning to read this book. Some of us do not like change because it is an unknown. It scares us because we are moved out of a comfortable, familiar place in our lives and compelled to move on. But change is a constant, and it will happen in spite of us. Some ways to enable kids to learn and understand these concepts of control, self-esteem, and change are to love them unconditionally, support and encourage them, be role models for them, and teach them some "stress management" skills so they can handle life on life's terms. There will be more discussion about change later as we discuss the many types of losses and transitions we experience along the journey and how they transform our lives.

2

STRESS: DO WE ELIMINATE IT OR TEACH KIDS HOW TO HANDLE IT?

Managing Our Stress Responses

Dr. Hans Selye, known as the "Father of Stress Studies," spent his entire medical career studying the effects of stress on the body. He gave us some very simple definitions, reminding us that stress is an inevitable part of life that cannot be avoided. He told us that stress is the body's automatic response to *anything* asked of it. The demand on the body may be positive or negative; the body responds in the same way. Blood pressure rises, the heart beats faster, our pulse rate quickens. Whether we receive a passionate kiss or hear a very frightening scream, the body's response is the same.

Selye also says we need stress in our lives to activate our immune system and stimulate the body into action. He called this the "fight or flight" response. More and more we realize we need stress so the body will be ready to lunge into action, for whatever reason. Stress has been called the spice of life because any emotion or any activity causes stress.

If we are sitting quietly in a room and suddenly there is a loud bang overhead, we will automatically jump. We were startled, but when we realize there is no danger, our body just relaxes again. This is the fight or flight response. Now we have a choice. Our body responded appropriately. Now what do we do? Do we start to yell and complain that the terrible noise disturbed our rest? Do we storm upstairs to find the culprit who made the noise? What we choose to do is in our power. We had no control over the noise, but we do have a choice now over our mental and physical response to stress.

Many athletes need and use stress to help get ready for their sports event. Many coaches are teaching their teams to visualize their run, picture their shots, or review their game plan in their minds before the event occurs. Business people are also visualizing their meetings, presentations, and sales events. This positive programming can help the person relax a little and usually feel a certain amount of confidence. As the adrenaline kicks in (the body's response to stress), the person is energized to begin the task.

☆ ☆ ☆

Nine-year-old Susie told us, "Before the meet, I get so nervous and my mind starts racing. As I dive into the pool, I start to feel the energy in my body and I feel very confident, relaxed, and ready to do my very best. The coach told me to make that initial feeling work for me."

☆ ☆ ☆

If we think of stress as needed and helpful, we can learn to adjust our responses, our perceptions. We can realize that stress is neutral, neither positive nor negative, and yet, very much a necessary part of our lives.

The body's response to any stress placed on it is the exact way the human body was designed to function. It is, as we mentioned, a sudden startle and then a calming down; a sudden response, and then recovery. Research is ongoing to study the body, mind, spirit, and emotion connection. We are total beings, not dissected into isolated parts. We now know that when we change a thought in our mind, there is a physiological response in the body. For example, if we were picturing a beautiful, calm beach scene, and then were asked to change that to a thought of anger or fear, there would be a real and physical response in our bodies. We also know that what is stressful for one person does not necessarily have to be stressful for another. We are gaining more information and insight through continued research and the use of biofeedback machines and other technology.

So if stress is needed, helpful, and the spice of life, what do we really mean when we say we are so "stressed-out"? Why do adults need to learn and practice stress management skills and why should we teach them to the children? The answer is because kids are stressed, too.

Distress

Selye describes the culprit as *distress*. Distress is a destructive force, filled with tension and turmoil inside "my" body or mind, brought about by "my" attitude, perception, or reaction to some situation. It is distress that causes upheaval within us because of our interpretation of and response to the event. Again, distress cannot be avoided in our life because situations happen over which we have no control. This is where we can help the children better understand this concept. We can clarify the term *distress* and teach them the skills needed so they can deal with stress when it occurs.

Selye and other researchers have emphasized that our attitude/response is what we can control; this will make a situation either more positive or negative. This is not meant to minimize the many tragic happenings or the sad events we must face. To better handle the distress when it happens, we are encouraged to name the reality and to deal with it using the skills we have learned. Many people seem to better handle the "big events" in their lives rather than the little everyday occurrences that seem to upset them so. It is through these everyday events that we can teach children about control. The key is to try and *respond* to a situation rather than *react*.

For instance, you drop a glass of milk. The milk spills all over and the glass breaks. You begin to rant and rave and call yourself stupid or some other unbecoming names that you do not deserve. Or you could respond differently. At first you are startled, but after assessing the situation, you realize that it is not a major tragedy. You respond, "Oops, it was an accident," and you clean it up without undue distress.

☆ ☆ ☆

We could continue this scenario by stating that the glass was a family heirloom, it was crystal, or it was irreplaceable. We may need to process this reality over and over, but eventually we will need to realize the fact that if we can't buy a new one, it is broken and it is gone. We need to acknowledge how this makes us feel, to feel the feelings; then when we are ready, we need to let go and move on. We are not in control of all of life's events.

If we continue to react or overreact in an upsetting manner, to even the most minor inconveniences, we are putting an added strain on our minds and bodies. If this type of inappropriate reaction continues, we can put our health at risk. Authorities tell us that the body has just so much energy to respond to daily events. When we squander it unnecessarily, we deplete this valuable supply; this in turn can affect or even lower our immune system. Constantly overreacting to situations, feeling impatience, anger, and a lack of forgiveness, can cause the greatest drain of our energy supply and can also have a negative effect on our body.

Lack Of Forgiveness Equals Distress

This depletion of energy is especially prevalent when it comes to forgiveness. A lack of forgiveness and holding on to hatred, anger, or other things that are no longer for our greater good, is a waste of our precious energy. Forgiveness is a distressful and very misunderstood concept. Forgiveness is a very selfish and a most beneficial choice we can make for ourselves. It is something we can do to free and release ourselves from the bondage and pain of being hurt. Forgiveness is not about saying, "it's all right what the person did or said" to hurt us. It is not about bringing those persons back into our life or telling them that they are forgiven. It is about a way of life, a way of being. Unless a person chooses to forgive and let go of the hurt, the pain will continue to hurt them, deplete their precious energy, and possibly cause some harm or *dis*-ease in their body. Buddy Hackett, a well-known comedian, has been quoted as saying, "While you are at home nursing your wounds, the other guy is out dancing." Either the person who wronged us does not even remember or could care less about what they did. They have continued on with their lives and we are the ones who are suffering. Yes, people hurt us. They may have abused us in some way. They may have said something that we perceived as hurtful. (Someone once said that more offense is taken than actually given on purpose.)

Other people have experienced outrageous hurts and irreparable atrocities. Some people remain focused on revenge, getting even, or punishing the other person. How long should we harbor this in our heart? How severe should the punishment be? What would really be the best revenge, or what would make us feel better and make up for the hurt? We have witnessed the results of revenge and getting even every time we see or hear of kids killing kids. These kids do not have the skills they need to handle hurt or embarrassment, so they get a gun or a knife and respond in violence. We need to help them find the appropriate words and actions to deal with the events in a healthier, less severe, less violent manner. Hurt can last for a limited time, but killing someone lasts forever; it cannot be undone. Other kids and adults have dealt with their pain or hurt, have been able to get through it, and eventually heal themselves. Even though a fistfight seems less dramatic than a killing, it is still just as inappropriate. We still need to start with very young children and teach them ways to solve problems rather than using violence of any kind.

Forgiveness is a choice, and this choice may have to be made repeatedly. It may take months to feel better, really let go, and release the person, event, or the pain. Jesus has asked us to forgive someone "seventy times seven" times. He is asking us to make a choice to forgive at least 490 hurts. We know that seven is a very biblical number. Jesus is asking us, no matter how many times we are hurt, to do the loving, Christian thing by forgiving the person who has offended us. Jesus knew how hard this would be because of our humanity. We may need to constantly ask God for the grace and strength we need to help us complete this process. Jesus was hurt many times, and yet he continually showed us that it was possible to forgive and release the pain. Jesus called on the Father to help him release the pain and forgive those who had hurt him. Jesus was hurt, yet, in his humanness he continued to choose to forgive the hurts, the denial of His friends, the fact that people doubted his word and teachings, and that some even wanted Him dead.

A lack of forgiveness blocks and destroys relationships. Jesus' way of life was relational. Through the love of the Father, Son, and Holy Spirit, we learn the message of Catholic teaching. That relationship teaches all of us how to love, revere, and respect each other. Jesus' relationship with his apostles and friends taught us another great reality: that with our faults, limitations, and imperfections, we are all still in process, striving for perfection, yet still worthy and deserving of love. Holding on to hurts and revenge distresses us. It blocks our relationship with ourselves. Forgiveness is holistic. We need to release and let go of what is physically, spiritually, and emotionally keeping us from being whole and in balance. It depletes our energy and is detrimental to our better health.

We have all heard the maxim "forgive and forget." I personally believe this is a fallacy. Research informs us that the mind is like a tape recorder or a biocomputer. All that we experience gets recorded in our mind; therefore, we can't forget it. In the case of a traumatic experience, we may use defense mechanisms to avoid, deny, or dissociate, consciously or unconsciously, from an event. My personal belief is that when we have full knowledge of wrongdoing, we can truly make the choice to forgive; we then will have no need to remember. It can be very painful to remember the hurt or event, so it is important that we have a supportive person with us. We have to feel the pain and release it, but we do not have to do it in isolation. Forgiveness is a real, healthy, and truly beneficial choice for our personal well-being. To forgive, release a hurt, and really let go is for us, for our benefit, not for the person who hurt us. Forgiveness is to do what Jesus did. It is a way of living as a real Christian, as a true follower of Christ. We can ask God to open our hearts and help us to forgive, release, and let go of whatever is holding us back from true healing.

Twelve-year-old Jason was "madly in love" with his girlfriend. One day, he and his best friend had a fight. Willie beat him up, which totally embarrassed him in front of the girl, and Willie stole her away from him. Jason was devastated, convinced he would never get another girl. Until he was twenty-nine years old, he continued to blame Willie for his insecurity with women and lack of female relationships. Jason constantly talked about and bad-mouthed Willie, spouting his hatred and vowing that whenever he saw him again, he would kill Willie for ruining his life. Jason and Willie went to different high schools because Willie's family had moved away. Jason didn't know that Willie died in a motorcycle accident when he was fifteen years old. Jason went to his ten-year high school class reunion and there he learned the news that Willie was dead. A friend asked him if he would finally let go of his hatred for Willie, forgive him,

and get on with his life. "No way, man," was his response. Jason carried his hurt, hatred, and pain for another year. Finally, a woman friend really laid the cards on the table. She said that it was about time that he grew up and took responsibility for his own failure in relationships. Jason eventually was able to understand that forgiveness was his choice and that it would free him to take charge of his life. A few years later, Jason and his girlfriend were married. Jason forgave Willie and freed himself.

More Self-Imposed Stress

In the Serenity Prayer, we ask to accept the things we cannot change and to acknowledge the things over which we have no control. Maybe we could incorporate this philosophy into our lives and teach the kids to pray this prayer many times daily. Besides worrying over spilt milk and holding on to a lack of forgiveness, another example of self-imposed distress would be fretting about waiting in line at the store. We could be impatient, waste our energy throwing a fit, fill ourselves with tension and upheaval, or we could stay calm. We could stay relaxed by saying a prayer or reading a magazine, acknowledging that our reaction is totally up to us. We could read the latest "research paper" that proclaims "Alien from outer space chats with the Pope." Our response, our attitude, will either make us more distressed or help us maintain an inner calm that enables us to handle the situation in a more positive manner. It will not make the cashier or the line move any faster, because we are not in charge. It has been recommended that if we only have a very limited amount of time, and, of course, if it is not an emergency, not to go shopping. We should wait until we have more time, or at least strive to acquire patience and be the star participant in the "waiting game." It is also a very good policy to always have a book (a novel, joke book, prayer book, word-search, or a magazine) with us whenever we know we will probably have to linger in some line or wait for the next available appointment.

Another way we distress ourselves is not making the time to get something fixed if it is not working properly. How often have we heard someone get extremely angry because something is broken? "These windshield wipers are driving me crazy! I have to get them fixed!" Maybe our child is complaining because his bicycle has a flat tire and "it is all your fault" that he cannot go riding with his friends. People in these situations continue to be aggravated and complain because they will not make the decision or take the time to get the "things fixed." This is the part of being in control where we have to make the choice and do something about a situation. Procrastination can be a source of distress because we won't make the decision to do whatever it is that we need to do. By making the decision to fix what needs to be fixed, we eliminate undue distress. Procrastination is not all bad, because it can also be used to scrutinize a situation, allowing time for an idea to ferment or take form in our mind; we then are better able to make an informed choice. For which purpose do we use procrastination? Does it lessen or aggravate our distress? It has been suggested that if we want to know how we handle distress, we should watch how the children closest to us react.

> *While driving down the road with the children in the car, someone cuts us off. What do we do? Many lessons can be taught and "caught" in this situation. Kids could learn the use of expletives, or they could experience our road rage or our road manners and courtesy. They could observe that we were startled by the other car and then hear us acknowledge this, or even pray that God would bless and keep the other driver safe and accident-free. What do we do in that situation?*

What do our kids learn in that scenario? Are we *actors* responding to the event in a healthy way, or are we *reactors*, triggered out-of-control by the episode? The children will "catch" this response from us; that could be their greatest lesson on how to handle distress. It would also teach them that a large part of stress management has to do with patience.

> *Daniel was four years old, and whenever things did not go his way he threw a fit, literally throwing things across the room. His mom was concerned about this behavior and finally asked him why he did that. Danny answered, "I don't know. Daddy did it."*

Danny had to be taught a new response to his being upset, and Daddy was urged to change his reaction, too.

Patience

Patience is a virtue and something we strive for to help us respond to situations in a better way. Patience helps us to tolerate the behavior of other people and encourages us to try and cope with their idiosyncrasies. No one is perfect—not even us. Each person has a distinctive way of being. Another person's mannerisms do not have to be like ours. There are different ways of doing things. When people do something that we do not like, or if they don't do things the way we want, we get angry. We lose patience when things do not go our way. We are forced to remember that we are not in control. This evokes that upsetting feeling inside of us and we do not like it. What can we do about it? Do we rant and rave and fight this reality, or do we take a few deep breaths, chill out, calm down, and acknowledge that every one is different and definitely in charge of their own choices. They do not have to do it "our way."

Another part of patience that kids need to learn is that all people are out to get their own needs met. People will make certain choices and they will do what they choose to do. We cannot make them do what we want. We can make a marvelous suggestion about something, but they are always free to choose their response. Now, this could make us very hurt and angry. We could try to influence them, try to make them change their minds. We could tell them how hurt we are, how they don't love us, because if they did they would do what we want. We could disrupt the relationship; we could "take our toys and go home;" we could scream, holler, and try to manipulate them, but this would not be healthy, loving behavior. They will do what they need to do. We are not talking about illegal, immoral, or bad choices. As long as their choice affects their own life and does not infringe upon us, they have a perfect right to follow the best choice for them, even if it was not ours. Of course, this freedom of choice does not pertain to tiny tots or young children who need limits and discipline so they can learn about self-control, consequences, and appropriate behavior, which will enable them as adults to make good, smart choices that will affect their lives. We are talking about friends, spouses, loved ones, or acquaintances, who may or may not have asked for our opinion, and about perfect strangers who are "bugging us" because of what they are doing.

We waste a lot of energy by being angry, bossy, or judgmental, and it usually puts an unnecessary strain on our bodies and on our relationships. We need to conserve our energy, breathe as deeply as is comfortable for us, calm down, take a time-out, count to ten, and try to practice patience so it will be available to us to handle the daily distress we encounter. We should not try to take control of somebody else's life, and should not try to change someone. There is a very strong message that Alcoholics Anonymous groups teach a spouse or a person dealing with a loved one's problem behavior. They call it the three C's: I didn't cause it, I can't cure it, and I can't control it. We should repeat this to ourselves many times daily. A person must choose to change because that person is in control. We can always pray and ask God to help us increase our patience. There is a story of a person who constantly prayed, "God, please give me patience and give it to me right now."

Anger

Anger is a normal emotion. The healthy release of anger can be very beneficial to our mental and physical health. As with many things, taken to excess, anger can cause injury, destruction, and harm to the self and others.

Researchers are investigating and debating the best way to handle anger. Some say expressing it vehemently can be detrimental, while others are investigating the core source of anger. Most authorities agree that to hold anger inside and let it build up is not a smart choice. This could lead to unhealthy and detrimental outbursts or some negative effect on the body. Definitive results are not yet known. They also continue to examine the cause of anger and violent behavior in children and adults. We can see little kids and big kids (grown-ups) angry because things are not going their way or they cannot have what they want. There seems to be a tremendous amount of anger and rage exhibited in our society today. The intensity ranges from "I can't open this package," to road rage and other violent, aggressive behavior. Younger and younger children are acting out their rage by beating up other kids or even just killing them. Why is there so much rage? What makes kids so angry and what can we do about it?

Eileen McGrath, Ph.D.

Researchers at Duke Medical School are studying the correlation between parenting/child-rearing skills and genetics. They are looking at the level of serotonin in the brain. Initial findings indicate that less serotonin accompanies more aggressive behavior. They also claim that poor nurturing as children can produce changes in the brain. As the studies continue, parents are strongly urged to demonstrate unconditional, positive love and nurturing to their children. Parents need the training to give a good example to their kids, especially if they did not have positive role models in their own early years. When the two-year-old throws a tantrum, instead of displaying parental rage or hitting the child, we should wait until the child realizes the tantrum does not get him/her what he/she wanted. Then we can soothe the child and help him/her to remain calm. Naturally, kids need limits, but they must be taught that "no" means no. They need to find words that will help them express their anger. They should be encouraged to talk about how they feel. For example, when Bob grabs a toy away from Jake, Jake needs to tell Bob that he did not like it, and that they should share and take turns. Other solutions need to be introduced to the child at each developmental level. This may sound bizarre or like an ideal situation, but the only way children will learn to change their behavior, to curb their anger, is if they are taught alternative methods. They can also learn there is a more peaceful way, a different choice, a better way to behave and resolve issues. This, of course, brings up the question of self-defense. Some parents have very strong beliefs about this area; it boils down to what

36

we have taught our child. Another whole book could be dedicated to this discussion, but for our purposes here, let it suffice to say that each of us must decide what to teach our children. We take into consideration our personal religious beliefs, our stance on violence, and what alternatives we could help our children learn. When is self-defense appropriate? What should be done and how children should handle the challenge of self-defense are questions to be considered very carefully, especially in our current society. Kids need to know the rules and that there are consequences for their actions. Our child may know our rules, but the other kid may have different ones or no rules at all. Our child's safety is our utmost concern.

Besides rules and firm limits, parents must follow through consistently with the appropriate response and discipline to fit the situation. Studies have shown that kids grow up and repeat their parents' patterns; therefore, a cycle of anger, aggression, and destructive behavior will continue unless today's youth can learn alternative responses.

Physicians and mental health workers are constantly warning us about stress-related ailments and diseases. High blood pressure, headaches, dizziness, stomach disorders, and backaches commonly head the list of complaints that may be indicators of distress in the body. These symptoms are found in adults, but today, pediatricians state that more and more children are manifesting these same ailments. Our children need to calm down and find a better way to respond to the distress they face. We need to help them by our words and example.

Eustress

Dr. Selye states we have the ability to use our skills and our faith to respond to situations in a healthy way and possibly turn them into blessings. He describes this as *eustress*. He uses "eu" to mean good, as in euphoria and euphoric. He asserts that the human spirit tries to make some sense out of life events. In this way, we become better people because of the way we handle situations and the lessons we learn from them. Tragedies do not happen to make us better people—tragedies just happen. It is our God-given spirit that helps us deal with those realities. Stress management is not about denying or repressing feelings. It is not about being a "Pollyanna." It is about naming and dealing with the different situations and coming through them in a healthy way.

Ten-year-old Amanda shared her story. "My dad lost his job. I thought it was the end of the world. I had to go to a different school, which I hated. I had to leave my best friends behind. I thought I'd never have friends again. I couldn't buy the things I wanted. We had to move to a much smaller house in some yucky town. It was awful." Amanda continued, "Eventually Mom, Dad, and I began to talk a lot, and we started to have more fun. Dad got a job nearby, so we had lots more "family time" together. I even made some new friends. (By the way, I called my old best friends and they didn't want to know me anymore.) I guess I learned that good friends will be there for *you and won't abandon you just because you moved. My family and I realized that the tragedy brought us closer together and changed our lives for the better."*

This family worked with their situation and seemed to handle it and come out a stronger family. Others are faced with seemingly insurmountable crises, but after time, work, their strong faith, and good philosophy of life, they, too, are able to pull through, adjust to their circumstances, and move on with their lives.

In my counseling practice, I have seen vivid examples of a person's depth of faith and unbelievable human spirit. For instance:

A young child was killed in an accident. The parents, although in the depth of despair and intense grief, wanted to donate their child's organs so that others could live. Because of their faith and courageous action, their child will not have died in vain.

Grieving the death of a child is a lifelong process; most parents will share that not a day goes by that their child is not loved, thought about, and missed terribly. Parents have said that the severe pain is lessened, but the scar will always remain. The poet Edna St. Vincent Millay said about those who have died, "the absence of their presence is everywhere." The memory of the person we loved will always be in our surroundings. They will always be in our hearts.

Some parents, in their attempt to make some sense of their loss, have dedicated their lives to helping others. These parents have volunteered to visit children in hospitals or raise money or start organizations for some children's cause. They know they will never get an answer to that haunting question, "Why, why my child?" but it gives them some sense of fulfillment to help others. Parents grieve deeply; they know their life is changed forever, yet they are able, after years of intense pain, to pick themselves up and continue on with their lives as a proof of their passionate love for their children.

Another example of the depth of the human spirit is seen in the many corporate men and women who were fired after many years of dedication to their careers and their companies. Some of them, now fifty-five or sixty years old, have worked through a very distressful period of depression and loss. They felt used and abused, their self-esteem plummeted, and some were despondent. Those who shared their stories related that they finally were able to pull themselves out of this darkness by relying deeply on their faith and trust in God and by using their skills to begin again. Some were able to enter totally new and different careers, and this has changed their lives for the better.

There are stories reported in the media every day about some real heroes, children and adults, who experienced a tragedy and have now turned their lives around. For example, there was a little boy who lost both legs when he was hit by a truck. He continues to play baseball, go to school, laugh, and have fun. He uses two leg prostheses and a wheelchair, yet when he plays ball, he uses only his hands and arms to propel himself around the bases. He is an inspiration to most people, but he also faces some ridicule from certain kids who are insensitive bullies.

We, as parents, teachers, and caregivers, hold part of the key to help kids develop and use their gift of the human spirit. Our attitude and the way we respond to loss and crisis in our lives will help them realize that with faith, hope, love, and support of one another, they can surmount all odds and go on living. There are two Chinese characters which are written the same way. One means opportunity and the other means crisis. When we are faced with a difficult situation, which meaning do we choose to help us handle it?

Hypostress

Dr. Selye gave us one other term that he called *hypostress*. This is too little stress or an actual deprivation of stimuli to the body. Usually, people who experience this type of stress are depressed and very lethargic. They have lost interest in normal everyday activities. They may feel hopeless, hapless, and helpless. These three "H's" have come to signify and provide the elements of some very self-destructive behavior.

☆ ☆ ☆

Eleven-year-old Billy believed he had absolutely nothing to live for. He felt he had no friends, and all

41

he wanted to do was lie on the couch. His favorite expressions were, "I don't care," and "I can't do it." Billy had just moved from the city into the suburbs and had started at a new school. The dress code was different; his clothes and his haircut were not like the other kids'. His mom couldn't afford a whole new wardrobe and he was certain his hair would never grow back. So Billy lied about going to school and played hooky. His mom had to leave for work before he had to leave for school. Since he had been in school only one day, it took a while for the school to catch up with him. Some kids had laughed at him that first day and he just felt he would never "fit in"; he was never going back there because "he couldn't handle it." Billy's mom finally discovered what was going on and she convinced him to see the male school counselor and give it another try. After some work with the counselor, Billy started to deal with his sadness over his losses and began to adjust to his new situation.

Parents and teachers of children with these symptoms should encourage them to talk about it, try to understand their situation, and then encourage them to deal with it. The children need help to boost their self-esteem and to learn some ways of handling the peer pressure and distress associated with moving or facing other new situations. Loss and change are very much a part of our reality, and caregivers need to be aware of and acknowledge that these experiences do have a psychological effect on kids. If talking about things doesn't work, the whole family (so the focus is not just on the child)

could seek help from a mental health counselor. Besides counseling, the children should be encouraged to do some form of exercise or movement. When someone is in distress, a relaxation response can be very helpful; in the case of depression or *hypostress,* one should be active, never sedentary.

Now that we have clarified and have a better understanding of the different definitions of stress, we can begin to identify some of the major causes of distress affecting the kids and try to discover where they need help with their lives. In this book, we will consistently use the word *distress* to name the inner turmoil and disturbance the kids may be expressing or experiencing.

The goal is not to shield them from distress, but to teach them effective coping skills and provide the other tools they need to develop a positive attitude, make good choices, and begin to feel competent and good about themselves. They need to develop the ability to distinguish between those things over which they have some control and other realities they cannot change. Children need to learn, at each developmental stage, to develop self-discipline, ways to better control their own choices, behavior, and emotions, and ways to handle the relentless pressures from peers and society. They need their parents' example and guidance to help them deepen their faith and trust in a loving God who is very much a part of their daily lives. Unless there is a change in perception and a different response to handling distress, they will constantly be frustrated and angry, and feel out of control. These negative reactions can only lead to feelings of insecurity and to inadequacy and a low self-esteem, and in many cases, self-destructive or anti-social behavior.

3

KIDS ON TRACK AND
KIDS OFF TRACK

Home, School, and Society

Teachers and parents want to help children successfully handle the many challenges in their world. Let's look at some of the major areas that cause kids distress, keeping in mind that adult perceptions are very different from those of children. We should also remember that all children are unique, and many are very resilient. Some of them, left to their own resources, have done extremely well in school and in life. They scored high on IQ tests, seemed to be more self-assured, adjusted to their situations, and moved on to good jobs and happy lives. Many other children developed and used different defense mechanisms and coping patterns to handle their individual life experiences. In some instances, these mechanisms did not help them to adjust to a healthy lifestyle and they grew into dysfunctional adults.

It is important to mention here that defense mechanisms are automatic psychological processes, usually developed early in life. The child does not even consciously know that this is happening; but it is the mind's protection against anxiety, or any major dangers or emotional distress. Defense mechanisms usually keep scary ideas, thoughts, feelings, and memories out of the child's awareness. Commonly, in the case of sexual, physical, or emotional abuse, or other trauma, these mechanisms protect the psyche from intense pain. Some very common defenses are avoidance, denial, dissociation, rationalization, repression, humor (an attitude that "nothing bothers me so I joke about it"), and "acting out" behavior. These defenses can make a child feel very safe and secure, but if he/she continues to use these mechanisms as an adult, they can stifle the individual and become detrimental to his/her psychological well-being.

Parents and teachers may become aware that some kids are "acting out" and using some defense mechanism to handle their situations. If we recognize any of these behaviors, we may want to have an open discussion with the children and/or their parents to discover what is happening, what help they need or want, and how we can be there for them.

The following sections identify home, school, and society as major areas where kids need at least some extra help with their world.

Causes of Stress in the Home

There can be any number of stresses on the life of a family, including the modern-time crunch, divorce, single-parent and blended family units, abuse, and family dysfunction, as well as losses due to illness and death. Families also experience difficult emotions such as depression and fear.

Sometimes "difficult," distressed children are acting out, misbehaving, or seeking attention because something "is going on" in their lives The typical all-American family never truly existed and can only be seen on old TV reruns and a few of the newer sit-com shows.

Today, kids must cope with the reality that both parents may work; many families may have very little time together or quality interaction. We know there are parents out there working very hard, in spite of their busy schedules, to maintain strong family values, a stable, loving, faith-filled environment, family meals, and quality time with their kids. They continue to hold the family sacred, providing opportunities for their kids to experience beautiful lasting memories that they will carry with them through life. But we also know that there are a variety of family structures in our society that have changed and will continue to change as we journey into the new millennium.

Modern-Time Crunch

A 1988 study by the University of Michigan Institute for Social Research found that working mothers spent an average of eleven minutes of quality time daily with the kids; fathers spent about eight minutes of quality time with them each day. On weekends, the time increased by two or three minutes. Ten years have passed, and the time crunch for some families is even more difficult and distressful today. Some parents are putting in 47- to 60-hour workweeks, which definitely impacts family togetherness. Although the quality time spent with kids now is still under 30 minutes, we are seeing a trend where fathers are getting more involved with their kids and with household chores. Some fathers have even left their six-figure jobs for less time-consuming careers, or become totally "at-home dads" because their spouses have a wonderful career and they want to spend more time with the children.

Many parents are "taxi drivers" or members of carpools for the kids. They rush home or leave early from work, pick up the kids, then drop them at sports practice, games, dance or music lessons, do errands, get the groceries, swing back to get the kids, and then try to relax as they prepare the meal as well as do homework with the children. For some families, the result of the fast-paced frenzy is that the daily schedule becomes unpredictable. There used to be a routine, a time for family meals, time for study, play, baths, and bedtime. This harried lifestyle can also affect the distress level for the kids. They are the ones participating in all these varied activities, and also being pressured by reports due, homework, study time, and household chores. Some experts believe this lack of routine could cause a sense of insecurity, frustration, and uncertainty in some children. Other experts may suggest this lack of routine could enhance a child's spontaneity and time-management skills, as well as help them develop flexibility. Definitive results are not yet available. So far, kids have reacted in positive and negative ways to their routines. A parent's attitude has a definite effect on the child's response to different schedules.

Mary Lou is an eight-year-old ice skater and third grade student. She gets up at 5:30 in the morning, grabs breakfast on the run, travels two miles to the ice rink to practice. She skates until 7:45 a.m., gets back home, showers, and walks three blocks to be in school by 8:20 a.m. She is an honor student, does her homework and studies from 3:15 until 5 p.m., eats supper, and is back at the ice rink for more practice until 9 p.m. Then home, to be in bed by 10 p.m.; the cycle repeats in the morning. When she was asked how she can keep up with such a schedule, she replied, "Usually it's no big deal. I love to skate, and only sometimes I get tired."

On the other hand, fifteen-year-old Margie felt that she was living life in the fast lane, just running on a treadmill and getting nowhere.

☆ ☆ ☆

Margie had a nineteen-year-old boyfriend, as well as a part-time job for a few hours after school daily and six hours each on Saturday and Sunday. She was supposed to continue her weekly piano lessons and also find time to practice, do her homework, baby-sit her younger siblings, and prepare the family meals. Margie started skipping her homework and playing hooky from school. When she was in class, she would fall asleep each day. All of this caused a decline in her grades. She stopped her piano lessons without her mom's knowledge. Margie just wanted to spend more time on the phone with her boyfriend or stay out late to be with him in person. She was feeling increasingly vulnerable, frustrated, and distressed. She began to smoke and drink with her boyfriend to try and handle the pressure. Naturally, things got worse and the drinking got out of hand. Margie refused to talk about it with her mom. She refused any kind of help because she could handle it herself. Margie also became anorexic. After many months on this downhill track, her mom and friends finally convinced her to go for treatment. This decision saved her life.

☆ ☆ ☆

There are too many Margies out there who need our help and intervention. When the pressure begins to mount, kids need to know there is an alternative rather than be crushed by pressure and start on a destructive downhill path. They need to learn the difference between being a quitter and becoming a "simplifier" who analyzes the situation and makes smart choices to eliminate some of the pressure from his/her life. If Margie had been able to explain to both her mom and boyfriend how she was feeling, she might have discovered another way to handle the pressure. She was not a quitter, nor was she a wimp. She had too much responsibility and too many things to do. Margie wanted it all—the money, activities, lots of time with her boyfriend. She was trying to juggle too much by herself. She needed help to realize that she was in charge of her choices. She would not disappoint anyone; if she did, they would have to get over it and respect how she was feeling. She would not, nor should not, be labeled a failure. Nobody else knew what she was feeling or what she was going through. Nobody could make choices for her that would affect her better health and her personal well-being. Older kids are in the driver's seat and they need our help to know when to back up, slow down, turn around, and stop. Actor Chris O'Donnell, well known for his roles in *The Three Musketeers* and *Batman and Robin,* was interviewed and quoted a 10-word sentence, consisting only of two-letter words. When he first heard this quote, it helped him tremendously: "If it is to be, it is up to me."

We as individuals can and must make those choices that are right for us, but we don't have to make them alone. It is a sign of strength to reach out and ask for help. Most people have heard the expression that when sadness, grief, or troubles are shared, they are diminished. It is a sign of growth and maturity when we are able to realize that we are not perfect, we don't have to do it all alone, and we are not islands. Sharing and communicating are important skills needed to carry us through life and enable us to make good choices and have healthy relationships. Unfortunately, because not all relationships last, even healthy ones, we need to teach our children how to handle the distress that comes from a change in a family relationship, such as divorce, separation from parents, remarriage, illness, or death.

Relationships

Healthy relationships are born, nurtured, and continue to grow out of real caring and mutual respect. Over the years, researchers have also found that a good self-esteem and good communication skills are needed to make a good relationship. Both parties must be capable of handling conflict and learning the give-and-take of compromise and sharing with each other.

These life lessons could be taught in school but they are "caught" in the home, as the children learn from example and are enabled and encouraged to practice these skills early in life. It is in the home where they first learn about relationships. Above all, God is relational. Through the Holy Trinity, we learn how to know, love, and care for one another as God has shown his love for us. It is through the beliefs and example of parents that children learn this basic truth. As they see this reality lived, they begin to absorb this practice of love, respect, and care for one another. If we help kids incorporate this into their lives, they can really have loving relationships in the future. One of the major causes of the breakup of a relationship is that couples give up too easily. They have not learned the basic premise to love, respect, and care for each other. Studies done over the last twenty-five years found the three major causes of marital breakup were a lack of real communication, a lack of conflict management or resolution, and sexual dissatisfaction. Even with all the self-help groups and books available, some people still have not learned these basic relationship skills. These three problems are still prevalent today.

Our kids need to learn how to handle conflict without fighting or violence. Many conflicts can be resolved by talking them through. Some conflicts over values may never be resolved, but it may be possible to find another solution in handling the situation without compromising one's inner beliefs. By sharing, listening, and understanding, conflicts can usually be handled calmly because each party receives new information about the situation. A certain level of maturity is needed to practice conflict resolution and to teach it to others. "Taking our toys and storming off," pouting, not talking to someone, and using the silent treatment are immature behaviors that will never lead to any resolution. Adults and kids need to learn the "win-win" technique. Nothing will be equitably or permanently settled if one person must win and be right no matter what, and therefore the other person must lose. A "win-win" means that an agreement or a solution can be reached even if both parties just agree to disagree.

Communication is a learned skill, even though most of us have been talking since age two. It is learning to

53

share what we feel, making "I" statements such as "I feel angry when you do such and such." If we start off with an accusatory statement like, "You make me so angry," the other person will become defensive and the anger in both parties will escalate. Communication is also about listening to what the other person is feeling. It has been said that is why we have two ears and only one mouth, to enable us to hear more of what is being said and to say less. It is always important to try to say what we mean and mean what we say. Often, conflict and miscommunication occur when we try to interpret what someone else has said when we actually do not have a clue. The only way to be certain is if we come right out and ask, "Could you tell me what you mean?" or "Could you say that again? I'm not sure what you meant." This is called clarification, and it is an extremely useful aid in communicating. There are courses and books that teach other skills for effective communication and conflict resolution. After we have learned them, we can then pass these skills on to our children.

One suggestion for adults is to listen, to tell the child, "I hear you," and if it is a good idea, to say so. If it is not feasible, say "we won't be able to do that right now," but thank them for their suggestion. The children begin to sense they are being heard, not ignored or put down, and this could encourage them to keep on sharing. Another point to share with the kids is the reality that if someone disagrees with *my* idea or opinion, it does not have to mean they dislike *me*. Everyone has and is entitled to his/her own opinion. It has been said that opinions are like noses: Everybody has one. When we express our idea, we don't have to be put down or feel wrong; it was our opinion and we had every right to express it. When we receive new information about a topic, we can choose to change our minds and also express our new opinion. If we could all have a good, healthy self-esteem and learn to communicate, according to Abraham Maslow, a noted psychologist, we would have the keys to life. We would not need everyone to agree with us and we would not feel so hurt or rejected.

Divorce

Some experts say that the average marriage in the '90s lasts about six years. The U.S. Census Bureau stated in a 1996 survey that the number of divorced persons has more than quadrupled between 1970 and 1996, from 4.3 million to 18.3 million. As the divorce rate continues to grow, it continues to have a definite effect on the children. Some kids seem to adjust and fare very well after the divorce. Others feel ashamed, depressed, and guilty.

☆ ☆ ☆

One nine-year-old boy told me, "I really believed I could bring my family back together, like it was before, but I couldn't. I failed. My mom and dad used to fight over me. It was all my fault."

Divorce must be explained to children as an adult decision so the kids can be guilt-free and not carry a burden of blame. The divorce was not their fault, even if the parents did argue about them or their differences in child-rearing techniques.

Some kids feel betrayed, abandoned, and angry. Some take out their anger on the parent who remains at home, even though it may be misplaced anger, because it feels safer. They could be really angry, but they do not want to lose their relationship with the parent who leaves. As one child put it, "I don't want him to divorce me, too."

Some kids take on the overwhelming responsibility to "take care" of mom and "fix" the chaos and upheaval after the breakup. Financial problems, especially for divorced women, become a tremendous burden, not only to them, but also to the children. Some kids worry about it incessantly. They should not really be privy to money problems, because it can cause the fear that they will not be taken care of or have the things they need. According to U.S. Census data gathered in 1993 and released in January 1998, millions of children are living in poverty in our country. The Children's Defense Fund reported in January 1998 that 20 percent of all children under the age of eighteen live below poverty level. This increase in the number of poor kids is attributed to the large number of single-parent households. However, the report also stated that, of all poor children, 68.8 percent are living in working families.

Psychologist Judith Wallerstein has done a 10-year study, and with some participants, a 15-year follow-up study, on the impact of divorce on 60 families, who together have 130 middle-class children. Five years after divorce, 37 percent of the children, while able to function each day, were experiencing emotional or psychological problems. It was expected that most would have healed and recovered by that time. Wallerstein reported her findings in her book *Second Chances: Men, Women and Children a Decade After Divorce.* She also noted that most children of divorced parents felt some fear and less protected. Many teenagers felt abandoned physically and emotionally. As the children matured and approached the time of their own marriage, their anxiety mounted. Their overwhelming fear was of betrayal rather than fear of making a commitment. Most children were affected in some negative way by divorce and the breakup of family life.

Over the years, I have counseled children who were adopted and then years later, their parents divorced. These kids expressed overwhelming feelings of anger, abandonment, and as they put it, "double betrayal."

Tony was adopted when he was six months old. As he grew, he was constantly reassured that he was special, chosen, and loved. His parents explained adoption to him as he matured. He loved his parents but was naturally curious, in later years, to learn about his birth parents. Tony was thirteen years old when he learned his parents were getting a divorce. He was totally devastated, furious, and filled with hatred, distrust, and rage. The normal hormonal changes of puberty were taking place, but this news intensified his anxiety. His parents

tried to reassure him that he was still loved and cherished, but Tony could not hear or believe a word they said. His self-esteem plummeted, he hated himself, and took the blame for everything. "It's all my fault. I should have never been born. No one wants me or could ever love me. What's wrong with me?" For several years, Tony focused on his "double betrayal." It took many therapy sessions and a lot of hard work for Tony to build up a level of trust in anyone, to rebuild his self-esteem, and to realize that none of this had been his fault. He kept struggling with, "Why did my birth mother have me, then give me away? Why did my adoptive parents pick me, choose me, and then leave me?" Tony is now twenty-two years old. He has worked through his anger, but his feelings of abandonment and being betrayed still scare him as he begins a serious relationship. He still works very hard trying to trust people. He has reconnected with his adoptive parents, even though they both remarried and have additional children of their own. Tony visits and joins in family celebrations. At first, he wasn't sure or denied he cared, but eventually, he searched for and found his birth mother; he has not yet found his birth father. He admits that he is being very cautious and taking things very slowly both with his birth mom and his girlfriend. Tony is healing slowly; he continues to work on understanding his feelings and the impact life events have had on him. On good days, he is able to joke about having double moms, double dads, and double families instead of focusing on double betrayal.

☆ ☆ ☆

Tony's story is unique, but in one way it does describe the impact that divorce has had on other kids. Naturally, different kids react differently. All children should be encouraged to deal with whatever feelings they are experiencing after the divorce of their parents. Divorce is an adult decision, and it does affect the whole family.

Single-Parent Families

The structure of the family is constantly growing and changing. As the high percentage of divorce continues, the potential for single-parent families increases. The paragraphs above discussed some of the physical, financial, and psychological reactions that can occur after a divorce. These are not entirely negative effects for some families since the restructuring of the family can be for the better. If the situation were abusive or dysfunctional, then some form of relief will probably be present. If parents are constantly warring with each other, or arguing over the kids or over custody, then sometimes the separation is seen as for the best.

There are an increasing number of cases where fathers have received full or sole custody of their kids, and the transition seems to be going well, from the limited reports we have to date. Joint custody also seems to be gaining popularity in different states, but definitive results have not been thoroughly researched. Reports from a few limited studies have claimed that joint custody doesn't seem to make any difference in the child's psychological well-being. In an experiment at Stanford University, Janet Johnson, a researcher, found that among 100 families studied, one-third of the kids were in joint custody and the rest were in sole custody. These researchers found that joint custody was worse for the kids, especially for little girls who may have felt hurt by the forced arrangements and scared by being away from their mom's protection. However, there are definitely joint custody arrangements that work out very well for the children because of the mature, amiable relationship between the parents. Judith Wallerstein and several other researchers now believe that the focus for children of divorce should be on their relationships with each parent and other family members. This focus seems to have the most important influence on their emotional health. Whether the mother or father is the head of the household, definite adjustments must be made by all those involved. There must be a reassessment of family finances, chores, child-care arrangements, parental cooperation, work schedules, and the scheduling of extracurricular activities. Women returning to the workforce definitely face a major adjustment.

In some recent statistics from the U.S. Census Bureau, the number of kids under the age of eighteen living in single-parent families has doubled in recent years. The Children's Defense Fund (CDF) reports also that female single-parent families make up 18 percent of all families and 54 percent of poor families. (It is a well-known fact that for most women, finances decrease tremendously after a divorce.) The CDF report continues by saying that 62 percent of women with children under six years of age, and 77 percent of women with children ages six to seventeen, are in the workforce. These numbers alone account for a tremendous amount of distress for both moms and kids. The constant juggling of schedules, work, child care, and quality time together takes its toll as some moms vacillate between financial needs, career satisfaction, and guilt. Quite a few moms in the workplace have mastered this challenge. They continue to blossom in their careers, find quality time to be with their kids, and handle the daily routine and distress with limited negative effects on their body, mind, and spirit. Personal satisfaction seems to play a positive role in reduction of distress.

Remarriage / Blended Families / Stepfamilies

Growth in the number of divorces and single-parent families parallels an increase in the number of remarriages. According to the Stepfamilies Association of America, about 65 percent of remarriages involve children from the previous marriage, so the number of stepfamilies is also on the rise. Remarriage and blended families can certainly add to children's distress. Some kids are extremely upset at the thought of a parent marrying again. For some kids it closes the door on their secret quest to reunite their parents and get things back to "the way it used to be."

☆ ☆ ☆

Nine-year-old Brian was very distraught when his dad even talked about remarriage. He felt betrayed again. After his mom left them, his secret dream and obsession was that it would be just him and Dad, alone, hanging out together, forever.

He inwardly felt petrified that his dad would abandon him, too. Whenever his father dated a woman, Brian would throw fits and constantly misbehave. When Dad found the woman of his dreams and talked of marriage, Brian went completely out of control. He ran away three times and attempted suicide twice. He was very nasty and obnoxious with his dad and his girlfriend. Finally, the father took his fiancee and Brian for family counseling. Brian finally learned that his dad loved him and was not going to leave him alone. He came to realize that he was not in charge of nor was he responsible for his father's or mother's choices. He had to deal with his feelings resulting from his mother's abandonment. He also came to realize that his father had to have his own life, too, and he could still be a part of it.

The adjustment period when two families combine is hard and, at best, a real challenge for all involved. The children must face the reality of new rules, possibly a new home and school, new ways of doing things, even the perceived or real display of favoritism by either the stepdad/stepmom for his or her own kids.

"I really find it hard trying to like or even get along with my new stepsister," said eleven-year-old Ellen. "She is ten years old and such a baby, a real brat. I told my dad how immature she is and he says just hang in there, it'll get better."

☆ ☆ ☆

Another child, seven-year-old Tommy, kept rebelling at the way his stepmother did things. "My real Mommy doesn't do it that way."

☆ ☆ ☆

Some other children claim that no matter what happens, the stepkids do get away with murder.

Thousands of blended families are united every day, some very successfully and others with varying degrees of distress or intense disruption for the kids. According to recent data from the Stepfamilies Association of America, one out of three Americans is now a stepchild, a stepsibling, or a stepparent. Children need to know what is happening and try to adjust to how this will affect *"my"* life. Through love, patience, and working together, some kids can regain their faith and sense of family and feel as if they really belong.

Kids should not be a part of one parent bad-mouthing or bashing the other. They do not have to be privy to nasty encounters or details of money matters. They need the information that will help them to deal with and adjust successfully to their new situation. Parents need to keep the lines of communication open and listen to their kids. The child should feel free and be encouraged to share feelings. These feelings should be heard and validated; later, suggestions could be offered to the child on how to deal with them. Parents could ask the kids for their ideas and recommendations on how to handle household chores or other suggestions of how they could all get along and function as a family.

Kids' opinions need to be heard. They need to be treated as individuals, respected for who they are, and have their feelings acknowledged. Parents (who are also adjusting) need to show children how to get along in this "time of blending" by their example, communication, conflict resolution skills, and patience. Great life lessons can be learned.

Grandparents

Another challenging reality today is that more than 1 million children live with grandparents who serve as the primary caregivers. Normally, grandparents have the luxury "to love, pamper, and spoil" their grandchildren, and are not forced into the disciplinarian or parent role. Having grandparents as primary caregivers can create numerous challenges and forms of distress for both sides. The grandparents, at an older age (or, in some instances, a relatively young age), with different child-rearing practices, living on a fixed income, possibly with some health concerns, are asked to start over again. These demands may take their toll. Additionally, the children may be rebellious or difficult because they resent or miss their parents, and may continuously try to take advantage of the situation. In some cases, however, the kids may be better off in this environment rather than with their parents. They may feel safe, have a loving atmosphere, a more stable routine, and a sense of family who cherish them.

☆ ☆ ☆

Six-year-old Kimberly was sent to live with her sixty-two-year-old grandmother, who was preparing to retire in a few months. "I love my Mimi," Kimberly told us, "but I really miss my mom." The situation was very chaotic back with her mom, who was neglecting her and was in a very bad situation with a boyfriend. When the mother and her boyfriend did come home, there was constant drinking, fighting, and abuse. The mother was only capable of trying to meet her own needs. Kim was just a bother and in the way. The little girl tried incessantly to please her mom. She did the dishes, cleaned the house, and tried to nurture her mom when she had a hangover or when she would stay in bed all day. Kim missed many days of school because education was not a real priority and she had to do the chores and play nursemaid. Even though she tried to handle the situation as responsibly as an adult, she was only a little girl. She so desperately wanted her mother's love, attention, and approval that she was willing to stay in this distressing situation. The school social worker visited the home and had the child placed in her grandmother's care. Little Kim had to learn that she deserved to be loved, nurtured, and taken care of; that she did not have to be the caregiver. She also needed to understand that her mother had to learn how to be a parent. Kimberly has not seen or heard from her mom in three years; she still lives with her grandmother. But Kimberly has begun to blossom because she feels loved, cherished, and nurtured.

☆ ☆ ☆

Some kids must live with their grandparents because of the death of their parents. After a divorce or separation, some adult children, accompanied by their own children, move back in with their parents because the younger family cannot make it on their own. Naturally, there are no perfect scenarios, and there are varying degrees of happiness in all the different family systems. As the structure of families continues to evolve, the children constantly need the loving adults in their lives to help them to develop the coping skills they need to make sense of their situation and their world.

Dysfunctional Families

Some children live in dysfunctional families where alcohol or drugs may be present. Much has been written about the devastating effects on children with addicted parents. Experts in the field claim that, without help, the child will grow into a dysfunctional adult and probably perpetuate the behavior. On the other hand, those who do receive help can and will change the pattern in their life and behavior.

In the dysfunctional home, there may be violence present, or physical, emotional, or sexual abuse that the child must endure, usually in secret and in silence. Excessive anger may be expressed by the parents or watched on many TV shows. Children learn their behavior more by example than what is formally taught. Violence usually begets violence; this is becoming the norm for a great number of children. Even if there is no excessive anger displayed in the home, kids learn it from their peers. Kids from very dysfunctional families need extra help to understand this disruptive family cycle and how not to perpetuate the same behavior. They will need to learn how to work through any emotional wounds, heal themselves, and try to get on with a healthy life. These kids need extra help with their world. Recent studies show that kids who are violent and abuse other kids have been physically or sexually abused themselves.

The reality is this: There are no perfect parents and no perfect kids. We hope all people will do the best they can with who they are, and use whatever emotional and psychological skills they have to be the finest family they can be. Parents and teachers can learn new skills when they become aware that their way is not working out. There are many books and training classes, written and taught by parents for parents, to learn new ways of effective parenting. A family cannot be perfect, but children have the right to grow up feeling loved and free of fear and abuse. They should never be the whipping post for adult anger or frustration. Children are our most precious natural resource and should be treated as treasured gifts from God. There are no perfect kids, and, as we know, they can be manipulative and very trying. They can push the adults in their world to the limit, and many parents and teachers succumb and give in out of exhaustion. As naughty and testy as some kids can be, they still need limits and still deserve a chance to develop in their world, to be protected, respected, taken care of, and loved.

Not all dysfunctional families arise from abuse. Some adults do not have the skills they need to be parents, so some children are products of neglect. They grow up without direction or encouragement. Some drop out of school and basically just drift through life. They have poor nutrition, poor hygiene, and limited ability or communication skills. Most states have very strict laws concerning the abuse or neglect of children. Every individual has the responsibility to report any suspected children at risk to child welfare, who will investigate the allegations.

4

HELPING CHILDREN
HANDLE LOSS

Realities We All Must Face

For all of us, loss is hard to handle. Times of transition and change, moving from one place to another, retirement, illness, divorce, and death can cause severe distress, and are all classified as losses in life. For children, loss can be quite inexplicable, and so they need extra help to deal with their grief, guilt, "magical thinking," depression, and fear. Children need to learn early on that change and loss are realities that we all must face.

From conception to death, we are constantly growing and changing. Kids also need to learn how to handle these changes they encounter. Although change is a constant, we do not like it because it causes dissonance and disruption in our pattern of behavior. As was said before, we get comfortable and feel secure in our way of life. Change disrupts this flow and may seem horrendous. But times of change can also be times of tremendous growth where we are called to extend ourselves and reach a higher goal, a new potential, and wind up being a better person. Kids need to be taught that change can be very positive and influential in their lives. Change can be painful, but not all change is terrible.

Illness

Illness causes change, and it is a form of loss. An ill person may lose the ability to function or may be unable to care for themselves. Some may change so much that they do not even resemble their former selves because of the severity, length, and debilitation of the disease.

Illness is a very distressful time, not only for the person who is sick, but also for the entire family. The sick person may need constant care, time, and attention. Even though this duty may be done out of love and devotion, it is an emotional and physical strain on the caregiver. This affects the routine of the family and can cause chaotic feelings. At times the turmoil arises because the caregiver is tired, distressed, or feels angry and takes it out on the kids. Most times the kids feel guilty about causing the upset and are unaware that the caregiver's reaction is not their fault. The kids were just being kids, especially if they were noisy, just being playful, or were seeking some attention for themselves. Some children are told it is their fault that the loved one is sick because they are too selfish or demanding. Other kids have been told that the sick person got worse or died because they were noisy and misbehaved. There are too many other kids who were accused of something over which they had no control. They felt guilty because they experienced multiple losses in their lives which they internalized and blamed on themselves. The following story is a true account of one little girl's journey through life and loss.

Grandmom was in her bed and she was very, very sick. Vanessa's mother and her two aunts went into the room. Mommy told two-year-old Vanessa to sit quietly on the stairs and be good. Vanessa was playing with her doll when it slipped out of her hand and rolled down the stairs. She lunged forward to grab it and began to fall. Vanessa screamed as she tumbled down and then lay crying at the foot of the stairway. The bedroom door did not open and nobody came out to see what had happened. All of a sudden the little girl heard a scream and sobbing noises coming from Grandmom's room. Her mommy came quickly out of the room and hurried down the stairs. As she came closer, Vanessa felt some comfort was at hand and held out her arms so her mother could pick her up and make her feel all better. Her mother was crying; she pushed Vanessa away and said through her tears, "You bad girl,

Grandmom is dead, and it is all your fault. I told you to be quiet." As the mother rushed by her to use the phone, Vanessa just sat down and cried. This precious little girl, seeking comfort for her pain, had no idea what happened; she grew into adulthood carrying this scene, as well as a tremendous burden of guilt, in her heart. Two years after Grandmom died, one of Vanessa's aunts died. When she was six years old, her mom and dad got a divorce. Four years later, her mother died suddenly and Vanessa went to live with her other aunt. Then, four years later, this aunt died, and she went to live with her father and step-mother. Vanessa was sixteen when her boyfriend was killed in a motorcycle accident, and only nineteen when her father died from cancer.

When Vanessa was thirty-four years old, she started grief counseling. She had planned to get married, but she was afraid and had broken the engagement several times. She believed that everyone she loved would die, and it would be her fault. Through her therapy, after years of emotional pain, feelings of abandonment, guilt, and an unbelievable history of losses, she was finally able to deal with the pain. She finally realized that none of these deaths were her fault; she did not have any horrible magical power to cause the death of the people she loved.

☆ ☆ ☆

That precious two-year-old was told (I have to believe) out of hurt, misplaced anger, pain, and distress that she was to blame. I also have to believe that her mother never meant to hurt her or fill that little girl with guilt. Many times very hurtful things are said in anger and distress, and even though they are not intended to hurt, much lasting pain and guilt remain in the heart of the listener. Vanessa bore that pain for thirty-two years.

Another type of loss associated with illness occurs when a child is not told what to expect. When someone they are close to is seriously ill, children need to know, on their developmental level, the nature of the illness. Is the person going to recover or is the person near death? Kids need to hear how very sick the person is, the fact that they may not get better, and that they may die very soon. Children are often told the loved one is very ill, but would never dream that the person would die. Kids have a right to say their good-byes or whatever else they want to say. If they know the death is imminent, they will have the chance to say those good-byes if they so choose.

Death

Death is part of reality for all living creatures. We are born into this world, we will live for a number of years, and then we will die. All those we love in our lives will also experience this cycle of life, death, and resurrection in Christ. No one can live here on the planet forever. All living things follow a cycle of birth and death.

Beginning in the Book of Ecclesiastes (3:8), Scripture tells us there is a time and a season for everything. A time to plant things and a time to harvest, a time to be born and a time to die. Our faith tells us that when we die, our physical life is ended, but our new life spending eternity with God has just begun. So, it is how we live and how we

73

love each other during the time we have here that will make our life worthwhile and filled with meaning. Developing an attitude to live each day as best we can, deepening our faith in God, and maintaining an appreciation of and a respect for life enhances our lives and is a wonderful legacy to share with our kids.

Guilt

Living our life in this manner would be the ideal, but we realize that is not always the case. People often place an additional burden of pain on themselves after the death of a loved one with regrets and remorse: "Why didn't I say good-bye? Why didn't I say I loved you? Why didn't I say I forgive you?" It has been said that regret and fear are twin robbers. Regret robs us of our past and fear robs us of our future. We need to teach kids to eliminate this unnecessary guilt that we put on ourselves, which is really a self-judgment. "I should have, I could have, if only I had, what if I had." These phrases are wasted self-talk because we did what we did out of love and with only our present awareness. True guilt seeks forgiveness and reconciliation. If we did something on purpose to hurt someone, then we must tell them we are sorry and ask for forgiveness. But the guilt that we impose out of regret is usually our way of judging ourselves and putting ourselves down, and we only feel worse. "If I had only been there, she wouldn't have died." Statements like this are not helpful; we call them "magical thinking." Behavioral psychologist Jean Piaget explained magical thinking as it might take place in the mind of a two-year-old. If the child wishes something to happen and it does, then the child believes it was because of some "magical power" she/he possessed, which is a classic example of magical thinking. Things will happen over which we have no control and we cannot take responsibility for someone else's life or death if we did not do anything to cause it. We are not in charge. If we were in charge all our loved ones would still be here, alive and well on the planet. It has been said that guilt is the gift that keeps on giving. Unless we release it, this "gift" continues to grow and haunt us throughout our life.

For our children, it is important to ask if the child feels guilty or feels that the death is in any way his/her fault. Kids take unnecessary blame for their secret thoughts or hidden wishes that may have been directed to the deceased. They may feel that something they did or said, or what they did not do or say, was the cause of death. The real cause of death should be explained to the kids at their age-appropriate level so that any misconceptions can be cleared up.

Three-year-old Nancy secretly told Grandpa that she hated him and wished he would go away.

Shortly after that he did die. This sweet little girl felt so bad, thinking she was the cause of his death. She held the secret inside of her until someone finally explained to her that sometimes we wish bad things on people because we are mad at them, but we have no secret power to make death happen by wishing it or thinking it.

☆ ☆ ☆

Kids need to know that sometimes siblings say "I hate you" or "drop dead" because they were having a fight. They need to know that sibling rivalry is very normal and sometimes members of a family will get mad, disagree, and fight, or even scream at one another. We need to help them understand that we still love one another even though we disagree so vehemently. Things are said in the heat of passion that can be very hurtful. That is why it is important to teach about conflict and forgiveness. Even if a kid wishes something terrible or says something negative to another, their words, although not charitable or nice, do not hold any magical powers to make the other person die.

We may also want to consider the relationship the child had with the deceased. A child may be extremely upset at the death of someone. The adults in his/her world may seem to be taking it lightly, or telling the child to stop crying and acting upset. Sometimes the person who died, though unrelated, was the primary caregiver or support person in the child's life. There may have been a close bond that no one else knew about. Adults must be models of grief so the children can learn that it is healthy, normal, and acceptable to express their emotions; that grief is a process that cannot and should not be avoided. We must reinforce for the child that we feel what we feel and that's OK. When we deal with what we feel, we can heal. They need to know that the intensity of the relationship usually determines the depth and intensity of the grief.

Grief

Kids need adult guidance to learn how to handle guilt and grief. When there is a death in the family, children "catch" their lessons about grief from our reaction and the way we handle or do not handle the situation. Do we talk about what happened and encourage others to do so? Do we openly show and express our feelings? Grief is an extremely distressful and emotionally draining experience. First of all, grief is a psychological necessity and will not just go away. It is just as normal and natural as sleeping, laughing, sneezing, eating, or feeling angry. It is a part of life. When someone that we love dies or is no longer a part of our life, we are usually sad, find it very painful, and we miss that person terribly. There is a saying that abnormal behavior in an abnormal situation is normal. People in grief usually find themselves acting in unfamiliar patterns, or experiencing things they do not usually experience. Since death does not occur every day in our lives (thank God, because we could not tolerate the pain), we claim that grief is an abnormal situation. What we and the kids need to learn is that whatever we feel is normal. We need to talk to kids about grief and death and let them know that they can ask any questions or express any feelings freely. Experts tell us that when death is discussed in a natural way, not grossly or morbidly, children can learn to accept it. An open discussion removes the cloud of fantasy or taboo. It is not healthy to hide death or try to shield the kids from it. Kids will find out about it and possibly receive misinformation or feel resentful because we did not tell them.

☆ ☆ ☆

A mother put her two little girls, three and five years old, to bed, went downstairs, and later died suddenly of an aneurysm. When the children awoke the next morning, they were told conflicting stories such as "Mommy is in the hospital" and "Mommy went away." They were not told the truth until two years later, when their behavior had become outrageous and very upsetting. They lived for two years wondering what they had done to make Mommy go away. They asked themselves if they were so bad that she never wanted to see them again, and if Daddy would leave them, too. The girls needed a lot of counseling and support to trust their father again and to begin to grieve, and to comprehend not only the major loss they had experienced, but also why they were acting the way they were. The girls said they knew something bad had happened to their mother because of the way their father and other adults were acting around them. But because no one had ever told them the truth, they kept wondering and feeling guilty unnecessarily for those years.

It is very important to help kids know that feelings of all kinds, including grief, just *are*. We feel what we feel. Feelings are also natural, healthy, and an integral part of who we are. When we feel happy, we laugh or smile, we share the feeling. When we feel sad, we may cry or just feel very down. This too, is a feeling, but many people hold their sadness inside instead of sharing it with others.

Sadness does not feel good, but it is an appropriate response. It is very normal to feel sad. It is also the time to cry when somebody dies, if that's what we feel inside. Tears are a very necessary function of the body. They keep the eyes moist, help clear out infection, and wash away any irritants. They are also a healthy response to what we are feeling. Some people cry when they are happy and others when they are sad or disappointed. Some people try not to cry because they were told at a young age, "I'll give you something to cry about. You are a baby and a wimp. If you start crying, you'll never stop." Tears are good. Recent studies have shown that the tears we cry when peeling an onion are irritant tears, but the tears we cry from some emotional response are filled with toxins. Toxins are harmful chemicals that are released from our bodies. Biochemist William Frey has collected tear samples and data on hundreds of men and women. He observed that the reason people feel better after crying is because their tears are removing chemicals that build up during emotional stress. Frey also reported that we may feel physically and psychologically worse by suppressing our tears. Margaret Crepeau, a psychiatric nurse, performed a study in Pittsburgh which showed that healthy people are more likely to cry and have a positive attitude toward tears than to hold them in and possibly develop ulcers or colitis, which are thought to be stress-related diseases. Children learn this suppression or release of tears through our example. Crying, sadness, anger—all emotions are appropriate when they are expressed in a healthy way.

Delayed Grief

A special note should be made about the reality that children may avoid, delay, deny, regress, and/or suppress their grief. Most kids do not have a strong tolerance for pain and they cannot sustain it for any length of time. They will go in and out of pain; at each developmental level they will revisit their grief and discover a new dimension to it or feel it more deeply. Grief counselors have discovered that kids who do not grieve, or who suppress grief, will find that it will and does surface at a later date.

Nine-year-old Kevin was extremely close to his grandfather. They traveled Route 202 almost every day going back and forth from arcades, the burger stand, the little league field, the fishing hole, and sports events they attended together. When his grandfather died, Kevin never talked about him and he seemed unaffected by his death. Everyone commented on how well Kevin was doing and how adjusted he seemed to be. No one ever really noticed that whenever the family went on an outing, Kevin would insist that he be in charge of the route they would take. He never wanted to travel on Route 202 and would get extremely upset if anyone even suggested it. When he was a junior in high school, Kevin's grades started to plummet and there was an obvious change in his behavior. No one put the pieces together to understand that the intense feelings that were surfacing were directly related to his unresolved grief over his grandfather's death, which was now manifesting

in his bizarre behavior. Finally, his guidance counselor asked him if he'd ever experienced a death in his family. This opened the gates to allow Kevin's pent-up grief and strong emotions to surface. Talking about his grandfather helped him understand his total dismay and his insistence on never traveling on Route 202. It also gave him new insight into his current behavior. The counseling helped him understand why he was feeling the way he was. Kevin was finally able to say good-bye to the grandfather whom he loved so intensely and begin the healthy processing of his grief.

Kids really need help handling all forms of loss and the emotions they feel. They need to know they are normal. We need not be afraid to talk about these things openly. Kids will pick up on our fear, discomfort, and hesitation. As we help them, we will find that through sharing our emotions, we will also feel better.

Emotions

Shock is usually an immediate response to death. Whether there has been a long illness or a sudden death, there is definitely a time of disbelief. Shock is the mind's way of allowing only a little reality at a time to enter our psyche. It is like a sieve, giving us time to catch our breath and not be totally overwhelmed. Some kids may act as if nothing has happened or they may seem not to care. They care. They are probably in shock and may not want to think about the loss. Some kids will use their defense mechanisms of denial or avoidance so they do not have to face the pain.

Anger is another strong emotion when a loss occurs. Kids could be angry at the person who died or angry because they feel the pain of abandonment. They could be angry at the survivors because they did not protect the one who died. They could also be mad at the doctors or medical community because they did not save their loved one. Kids need extra help in handling anger and learning healthy ways to express it.

How can we help our children? We need to know their personalities. Are they active? Would it be helpful for them to run, punch a punching bag, play racquet ball, ride their bike, punch a pillow (always aware that they should not punch others or walls)? What active way could they use to express their anger? Some kids are more subdued, so they can get out their angry feelings by writing or drawing. Keeping a journal or writing a letter to the person at whom they are mad, whether they are alive or dead, can be therapeutic. They can use the letter to tell the person how angry they are. These letters do not have to be mailed. They could be read out loud to an empathetic listener or ripped up into tiny pieces and thrown away. Some kids take a crayon/pencil and scribble on a large piece of paper or draw circles or just scratch hard lines up and down the page. We can encourage them to talk out loud and express their anger: "This is for the time you did this, this is for the way you did not help, I am so mad at you because," and so on. Anger is real and needs to be expressed in an appropriate fashion. Helping children explain why they feel angry may also help them to release it.

Another strong feeling kids have is that of deprivation. They feel an empty void because the person they
loved is no longer with them. Some kids, and adults too,
may start to steal, or use and abuse drugs, alcohol, sex, or
food to fill that emptiness. Kids need to know how to
grieve, feel those painful feelings when they surface, and
realize it will take time and work to get through the pain
of loss. They need help to know that things will be
different, but that every effort will be made to try and
keep things as normal as possible even without their
loved one. They also need to realize that their loved one
will continue to live on in their hearts and memories.
The truth is that love does not die; it is expressed now in
a different way and no one can ever take it away.
Children need to know that any self-destructive
behavior will only cause added pain and suffering. Their
misbehavior does not prove how much they loved the
person who died.

Depression

Some form of depression can be expected after the death
of someone we love. Kids are not exempt from this
emotion. Some kids experience depression when there
has been no apparent loss due to death or divorce.
Authorities now realize that depression is more prevalent
than previously believed in younger children. This type
of depression is attributed to the children feeling helpless
and hopeless. They feel there is no way that they are
going to be happy or will ever get out of their present
situation; thus, some feel despair.

Suicidologists have informed us that kids as young as three years old have manifested signs of severe depression and have attempted suicide. Some kids aged six or seven have succeeded in taking their own lives. A seven-year-old girl decided to end her life because "Life is boring. There is nothing to live for." Kids with severe depression should receive help as early as possible. They need to know that there is help available for them. If it is a biological or chemical depression, they can receive medication and therapy that will help them feel better. They need to be taught that suicide is not an option—it is a very permanent solution to a temporary problem that can usually be worked out. We can help them to understand that whatever is bothering them needs to be talked through and handled so there can be a better solution. Again, they need to know they are valued, loved, and very important to those who love them. If they are feeling unloved—and this seems to be the major problem—then people can be found who will love them and treasure them for who they are. That is why we have foster care and adoptions. These are viable alternatives, and there are also other options available to them.

Thank God that all kids who feel some level of depression are not suicidal. They are basically feeling very down, and they need our help to find out what is causing this feeling. Some authorities say that depression could be anger turned inward. Counseling or a sympathetic listening ear from someone they love and trust may be just what the child needs. When feelings are shared, pain can be diminished. There is an area of psychology known as cognitive therapy. Its basic theory is that we are constantly talking to ourselves, and those thoughts can either build us up or tear us down. Much has been written about this self-talk and the belief that we cannot afford the luxury of a negative thought. Cognitive therapy helps a person to be aware of the messages they are giving themselves and teaches concrete, systematic steps to change these thought patterns. This is a simplistic explanation, but we can teach kids the danger and the effect negativity has on their attitude, their minds, bodies, and emotions. Parents, teachers, and caregivers must be aware and alert to recognize any major change in mood, attitude, or behavior of the kids in their care. Early intervention is a must to help kids deal with any signs of depression.

Fear

Fear and anxiety are very much a normal part of growing up. At different stages of development, kids sometimes experience irrational or unreasonable fears. Fears of the dark, monsters in the closet, lightning, strangers, germs, and going to school are some of the age-related fears that will pop up. These fears seem to be short-lived and very transient. Most parents can calm the kids, check the room for aliens, leave a night-light on, and assure them that they are safe. Other times, fears and anxieties can surface because there is something going on in the family. As a counselor working with families, I have seen children manifest certain fears or physical symptoms as a definite response to upheaval in the family and to parental arguments. One child would always complain of pains in her stomach every time her mom and dad were yelling. She would actually come downstairs, stand between them, and cry from her stomach pain. The parents would stop the fight and try to help her find some relief from her discomfort. Other kids have had migraine headaches; if the pediatrician found there was no physical cause for the symptoms, he investigated the parents' relationship. Kids are peacemakers and matchmakers. Sometimes trying to keep peace at all costs plays havoc on the little ones and they end up paying the price.

One little girl would actually get a pain in her stomach and vomit every time her uncle came to visit. It was later discovered that he was molesting the girl.

Seven-year-old Tommy woke up each morning in October with diarrhea and nausea. He did not want to go to school. The teacher discovered that four 5th-grade bullies were taking his lunch money and threatening to beat him up if he told anyone.

Four-year-old Joshua would have an asthma attack whenever his mom would start drinking after lunch. The doctor discovered that the boy's mother was an alcoholic who would get violent after drinking. No wonder little Josh was petrified.

So how do we know when the children's fears are normal, unfounded, or directly related to disruption in the family or in school? First we should look at the age of the child and the intensity and duration of the fear. Most normal fears will dissipate within a few months or within a reasonable amount of time. If the anxiety continues or becomes obsessive, or if it reaches the level of panic attacks and begins to interfere with the child's development or function, professional family therapy is recommended.

Some kids will try to cover up their fear because they want to be tough and not be considered a baby or a wimp. If these fears are held inside, we may see certain changes in their behavior. Their schoolwork and grades may plummet; they will not want to participate in normal activities with their friends or peers; they may manifest psychosomatic illness and sometimes experience full-blown panic attacks. The kids need help so they can understand there is conflict in a normal relationship. They are not in charge of their parents' dispute, and they need to find an alternate way to handle this anxiety without having it manifest in their bodies. If the tension is in school, where kids are stealing their money or hurting them physically, they need to report it to a trusted adult so it can be dealt with. No one will have to know that the child reported it, and he/she will be safe from retaliation.

The childhood fears just discussed are more normal than not. There is a greater fear that kids growing up today face as part of their daily reality. They realize they live in a scary, sometimes even dangerous, world. Latch-key kids may view hours of TV, using it as a companion to help obscure scary sounds or just the thought of being alone. Kids hear stories of bombings and shootings in schools and in the workplace. They worry over baby-sitters and feel anxious listening to the news on TV. Even looking at the milk carton on the table, with the pictures of missing children, could fuel a secret inner anxiety or an outward cause of apprehension.

Thirteen-year-old Tammy says, "I sure am scared. We hear about kids getting killed or raped or disappearing. I sure don't want that happening to me."

For many children the fear is very real. Violence is a reality they see all around them. When a tragedy occurs either in the child's immediate environment of home, school, and neighborhood, or even on national television, the children need to be able to talk about it. It could be done in a family discussion where each member is encouraged to share his/her feelings, which would be listened to and validated. The school could offer assemblies, or provide classroom or small-group discussions. Individual counseling should also be available. The proximity of the crisis would determine the urgency and intervention that should be provided. We will talk more about the school crisis in the next section.

Limits

Constructive discipline is another way to show love. Children need rules, guidelines, and limits on their behavior that help them prepare for the world around them. A spoiled child will grow into a spoiled teenager and a spoiled adult. They will enter a world that will not respond kindly to their tantrums or give them everything they need or want. Children need consistency and clear direction. They need to know that we mean what we say and that the discipline will match the deed. Children are really in charge of their choices. Parents cannot be with them every single minute, so the sooner they learn to be responsible and make smart choices, the better. The sooner kids learn that with every choice there is a consequence, it may help them to make better choices, be better behaved, and feel happier within themselves.

Choices and Consequences

Consequences and punishment are really quite different, although as a child first experiences them, they may feel the same. They need to understand that if they choose to do A, a bad choice, then B, the consequence of that choice, will follow. This type of instruction is part of an excellent program for parents called STEP, Systematic Training for Effective Parenting. This program, written by Don Dinkemyer, will help parents learn and practice this concept of choice and consequence training and other successful suggestions for parenting. For example, if children are misbehaving at the supper table, they can be told they have a choice. They may stop the behavior and eat their food, or they may leave the table. If they choose to leave the table and later on that night they are looking for a snack or treat, they will discover that their choice to leave the table means nothing else to eat tonight; maybe they could have a treat the following night. Another example is the child who wants to go outside without a hat or gloves or with an open coat. The natural consequences of this choice are that the child will feel cold or uncomfortable and eventually will put them on. (I can hear parents worrying the kids will catch cold, they will be hungry, they may get sick. This concept is in no way meant to harm or endanger the child.) There are many other examples and recommendations made by professionals and parents who have mastered this concept.

This choice and consequence stance is very hard for parents to maintain while the child is learning this life lesson. But it is just that, a lesson for life. If kids can learn this early on, then it becomes a habit for the future. They will take responsibility for their actions. This excellent plan also benefits the adults. They will not have to rant and rave, or scream, or argue repeatedly for the children to behave. This also works very well for teachers. The parents can tell the child, "You have a choice," and the parents can remain calm and lower their level of distress and frustration. For example, if a parent asks the children to clean up their rooms and they ignore the request, what will happen? The children could be grounded or punished, or they could be told they have a choice. They decide not to clean it. An hour later when they ask if we will drive them somewhere or give them money for the movies, we can calmly respond, "I asked you to clean your room, you made a choice not to do it, so my choice is not to take you or give you the money. Maybe tomorrow you could ask me again." Remember, there are no perfect parents or kids, so this will take patience and practice. Of course, the operative word here is "consistency." Kids will not learn this immediately, but after experiencing the consequences a few times and seeing the change in our behavior, they can and will get the message.

Kids cannot have adult supervision twenty-four hours a day, every day of their lives, so when they are on their own they need the tools to control their own behavior and to have well-developed, problem-solving skills. When they start to make a choice, their inner conscience reminds them and their sense of responsibility kicks in, and, we hope, they make a smart choice. Some parents, in an effort to spare and protect their kids, have let love blind them. It is a good rule to never make excuses for our child's behavior. Helping children take responsibility for their actions helps them to develop a conscience, inner control, empathy, concern for others, and good moral behavior. These seem to be the tools some kids are lacking today, thus resulting in the violence in society, the lack of respect for other people and their property, and the lack of reverence for human life.

Discipline

It should be said that discipline is a tool to enable children to be in control of their choices, not an instrument of torture, abuse, or cruelty. Some parents reported that they occasionally spanked a young child (one quick, light, hand-slap on the child's bottom), but more often they gave him/her a time-out or sent the child to his/her room. Most parents instruct their kids not to hit others, so if the child gets hit by the parents it sends a conflicting and confusing message. Discipline is also a sign of love so kids don't think they can do anything they feel like doing, like hurting others, or destroying their own or others' property.

According to parents who have successfully raised their children to become relatively happy, healthy, well-adjusted, and successful adults, a child should never be beaten or hit out of parental rage. Time-outs, removing toys or some favorite game for a limited time, revoking computer time or TV privileges for a length of time appropriate to the behavior and age of the child—all are constructive discipline. A time-out for a toddler can be measured by turning an egg timer upside down and telling the child that when the sand is all at the bottom, the time-out is finished.

As we said above, kids are out to get their needs met. They need our attention and they need us to listen to them. They also need quality time with us, talking, playing, reading, sharing family games and outings, and building treasured family memories together. Love them, cherish them, respect them, first and foremost, because they are a gift from God and we are God's co-creators. Second, this nurturing will enable them to be happier, healthier, and better armed to handle the distress in their lives.

5

STRESS AT SCHOOL

Power of Positive Students

The school environment can be a haven in the storm for some children; for others, it is another place of distress. Researcher Bill Mitchell wrote a book entitled *The Power of Positive Students*. As part of his research he discovered that 80 percent of kindergarten children entered school with a healthy self-esteem. By the time those same kids were in fifth grade, only 20 percent had a good self-esteem; by the time they were high school seniors, only 5 percent had a good self-esteem. We are not saying the school system

destroys self-esteem in children. As mentioned earlier, a positive self-esteem is a lifelong journey and it is affected by well-meaning adults, peers, anyone significant the kids encounter. Self-esteem is one of the keys to life. Building self-esteem needs to be a deliberate endeavor by parents, teachers, and caregivers, and, eventually, the individual. It must begin in the home where kids learn and begin to know and believe that they are unique, special, lovable, and very capable. They cannot be compared to a sibling or anyone else because they are truly one of a kind. They need to know they were created by God, and God threw the mold away because each person is unique. Through love and concern, they will know and feel that they are cherished for who they are with their individual personalities, gifts, talents, and limitations.

Schoolteachers have to truly love teaching because they constantly encounter imperfect, impatient, and needy little kids with their gamut of personalities, abilities, and potential. They experience some kids who are disruptive, disrespectful, messy, or who, by being just obnoxious, push the limits as hard as they can just to test the teacher's patience. They also experience the wonderful, well-behaved, cooperative children, those beautiful angelic faces just hanging on their every word, ready and eager to learn. Teachers know their students come from a wide variety of family structures, backgrounds, and cultural experiences. Many kids have been exposed to day care, preschool, or pre-kindergarten, so by age five, when they enter elementary school, they have already learned certain skills and behaviors. Different caregivers and teachers have diverse ways of handling and teaching the kids. Some of the children appear to be very set in their ways. A lot of them seem smarter and more advanced than kids entering kindergarten years ago. Some of them are computer wizards, or they can read, and many may be far beyond the nursery rhymes stage. Their experiences of previous childcare situations and their successes there will determine their degree of apprehension entering a formal classroom as well as affect their level of comfort or distress.

Teachers are virtually in charge of the classroom environment where children will spend more than 1,000 hours a year for twelve to fourteen years. Their influence is absolutely unequaled. Teachers set the tone and the stage for learning, enabling children to succeed and feel good about themselves. Teachers can help build a child up or literally tear a child down. They can provide successful experiences for the child where any task completed can be an accomplishment to be celebrated, or the child could experience frustration and failure. The school environment gives kids practice in meeting the challenges and demands that they will encounter in life. It is here they will continue to learn how to cope with disappointment, handle some frustration and possible distress, and also experience some level of enjoyment and success.

Teachers are copartners with parents, constantly building the bridge between school and home. The more connected parents and teachers are, the more the children can feel cared for, loved, and safe. Teachers also represent adult authority to the kids. That is why the classroom needs limits and well-defined rules. Parents and teachers must continue to support each other and never undermine one another's authority. If the children know that parents will back up the teacher's recommendations, then the children's classroom behavior should improve. Limits help children develop self-control and create a more predictable environment where the children feel safe and secure.

Kids, Guns, And Violence

Even as I write this book, children are experiencing insecurity and fear. Violence, tragedy, and murder are taking place in some of our schools. Some children are killing or wounding other children and teachers. Metal detectors and security guards are greeting children at certain school doors instead of the principal. The kids are being searched for weapons and drugs instead of chewing gum. A recent statistic claimed that about 1 million children brought guns to school last year. This, of course, raises the issue of gun control, the reality that stricter laws and other state regulations are required that will make guns less accessible to kids. It was noted that of the guns confiscated by the police in New York City, 1 in 9 guns were taken from kids less than eighteen years old. When children were interviewed in different sections of the country, most kids knew where to get a gun, how much it would cost ($35–$45 depending on the size and caliber), and how easy it is to get a gun or even a semi-automatic weapon. President Clinton has proposed a law that gun-owning adults would be fined or otherwise punished if their weapons were not securely stowed and became accessible to children who used them for violence. On the other hand, there is a national campaign by gun supporters that says, "Don't eliminate, educate. Teach kids a healthy respect for guns." What we need to teach them is that guns are dangerous and that we do not fight or solve our problems with a gun. There are other and better ways to handle disagreements.

Some kids no longer feel safe in their hallowed halls of learning. They are experiencing fear and anxiety along with their peers because of harrowing incidents in their environment. Some school cafeterias, instead of being places of nurturing, camaraderie, and socialization, have become places filled with fear, apprehension, and wonder. Could it happen here? Would a student ever open fire in school? Is the playground safe and a place of recreation, or is it to be avoided for fear some kid will "flip out" and start shooting an automatic weapon? Many kids across the country are asking these very same questions. Yet, kids seem to have two very opposite opinions when it comes to guns. Some kids insist that they must carry a gun for protection. They believe that guns mean power, success—and that violence works. This group believes that guns are to be glorified, because they imagine that guns confer attention and respect. This, of course, is a fallacy: it is not respect, but fear. To these kids, it feels good to take revenge or use a gun to get even. These are very scary thoughts and produce much distress in other kids who hear their peers talking like this. The other group (thank God, the majority of kids) believes that guns are not only dangerous, but should also never be in the hands of kids. This group believes that disagreements can and should be settled in a less violent way, especially by using problem-solving techniques and by talking out their differences. They don't respect these other kids; as a matter of fact, they think they're real losers.

When school authorities hear of violence, a hostage situation, or a murderous episode involving children in some school, they do not ignore it. The kids are very aware of what is going on around them, and they would have a heightened sense of vigilance and anxiety. School staffs continue to provide assemblies, small group or classroom discussions, and, where needed, individual counseling for the children in the most distress. Periodic "reality" or "anxiety" checks are spontaneously taking place or are being built into the school schedule so kids know that they have an outlet or a way to vent their fear and concerns. Thank God, there are still many schools that have had no outbursts of violent behavior.

Problem-Solving

School personnel, in spite of the violence and death that has invaded some schools, are still working tirelessly and diligently to make the classroom a safe place of learning. They continue to try and make the kids' everyday experiences as normal as possible.

As the school day progresses and the lessons are taught and learned, there are definite moments of normalcy and even some fun for the children. That is why a schedule or a routine is very important for them. This helps kids to organize their day. Some of them, because they know what to expect, feel more relaxed, secure, and able to immerse themselves in their activities. Other kids have used their marvelous defense mechanisms and have simply put fear out of their minds. When they arrive in school they focus their attention on the task of the moment. They really do enjoy learning, and they have fun in class, especially at gym and lunch. They are truly kids just being kids. Their laughter is contagious and they have a good time. Some are still self-appointed class clowns, of course, doing mischievous tricks, making annoying sounds, or just talking and causing the teacher major distress. For some kids, discipline is good because at least they are getting some attention, even if it is negative. Most of the kids that are "acting out" really do need the attention, so it is a good policy, where possible, for teachers to surprise these kids with some positive, unexpected praise because they are sitting still or paying attention. Usually, misbehavior indicates some deeper problem going on in the home or in the child's life.

Every curriculum should include problem-solving techniques. We would hope that these skills were taught in the home so kids can learn ways to handle and resolve problems without violence. Kids need to learn values, empathy, and respect for one another. Kids are exposed to the violence exhibited by their peers and a high-pressured society. If they do not learn and develop empathy and morals, they will not develop a conscience. Without a conscience, kids cannot and will not take responsibility for their actions. Without empathy, a child has no respect for human rights or a person's feelings or an animal's well-being. Theodore Roosevelt said, "To educate a child without morals is to educate a menace."

A Healing Presence

Teachers are still loved by many kids. Teachers play a vital role in providing support, understanding, and empathy to those kids who are experiencing tremendous distress and upheaval in their lives. Besides the obvious fear of violence, some kids are still very much in their own world of pain, grief, or sadness because of what is happening in their homes or families. Many of them are dealing with some of the distressful realities mentioned earlier: divorce, death, or abuse. Some of them are still reaching out to their beloved teachers, who are there providing a listening ear and words of encouragement and hope. Some kids feel that parents are not listening to them, so they turn to another adult to be their mentor.

Teachers must remember that they are not miracle workers and they will not be able to solve all the kids' problems, especially when they stem from the home. If kids are grieving a divorce or a death, it helps to remember they cannot short-circuit the process and we cannot take their pain away. They need to feel and walk through the pain. It may take them a year or two before they feel like themselves again. There are no easy solutions or answers, but our being there for the kids is the best gift we can give. Teachers can truly be a healing presence for them in a seemingly sick and troubled world.

Role Models

Many communities are investing in mentor programs and afterschool activities for kids. Big Brother and Big Sister programs are becoming more popular and are very effective in helping kids know that people do care about them. They can spend precious time with these mentors who can teach them valuable skills through sports, problem-solving techniques, limits, and choices. Television stars and athletes are doing TV spots urging kids to believe in themselves, love themselves, to say no, and stay away from drugs, spray cans, alcohol, and sex. Mentors who are aware that some kids are sexually active can reinforce the concept that kids should not have sex, and especially unsafe sex. Abstinence is still the best and safest practice when it comes to kids and sexuality. School sexuality programs, parents, and mentors need to remind kids to just say no. Young kids who are sexually active place themselves in very dangerous and difficult situations. Besides the threat of sexually transmitted diseases, they face the reality of parenthood. Kids having kids or kids being faced with extremely difficult decisions about their babies are painful realities that alter lives forever. Most people value life and believe that abortion is not an option. Unwed mothers (or any pregnant female) are strongly encouraged to put their unwanted child up for adoption as a definite viable alternative. To bring a child into this world is an awesome responsibility, one that most kids are unable to handle. This entire book speaks of distress, pressure, and the reality that all kids need a stable home and a mature, loving, caring adult who will guide them on their journey through life.

Peer Counselors

A large number of schools have initiated programs that train kids to participate in peer counseling and peer mediation. These programs seem to be effective in helping some kids find relief from their distress. Kids who need to talk, or who are experiencing some problem that they do not wish to share with an adult, are taking advantage of these peer programs. Of course, the peer counselors and mediators are trained to spot or listen for potentially dangerous or emergency situations. They then encourage the student to go to a teacher or counselor so they can get the professional help needed. If the troubled kid does not want to seek help and talks of violence to self or others, then an emergency intervention is needed. The peer counselors/mediators are strongly advised to tell the authorities. Police have analyzed the histories of some of the kids involved in the recent shootings and found that many of them talked about getting even or getting revenge by obtaining a gun and threatening to kill people. When anyone hears this kind of talk, it is imperative to tell—it is not an option to ignore what these kids are saying. Our first loyalty is to respect, value, and protect human life.

The values and skills learned in the home and continued to be nurtured in school are the tools the kids will need as they take their place as mature adults and viable members of society. The unconditional love and education we give kids today will determine the quality and strength of future generations.

6

CHALLENGES FROM SOCIETY

Causes of Stress in Society

Our kids must face many challenges today in a society of constant flux and rapid change. We live in an age of instant gratification, instant food, instant communication, and the unrealistic expectation of instant success. Different fashions, lifestyles, and moral behaviors are being reviewed openly in all forms of the media. Headlines are constantly revealing some person's private life. Sexual and marital infidelities are being reported daily, some repeatedly. Drug and alcohol abuse are aired in the open, or treated as comic relief or as material for nightly monologues on talk shows. Sacred values and morals, even individual indiscretions that were not discussed previously except within the intimacy of a relationship or the Church confessional, become the opening story of the nightly news. Daytime television and prime-time shows, which children are watching, are displaying indecent, and often times abnormal, behavior from people who probably would benefit from psychiatric intervention. All in all, our society has definitely changed over the years. Let us explore some of those societal changes and the effects they have on kids' distress levels today.

Lifestyles

A great deal of childhood distress is a direct result of the shift in lifestyles in our country. Many working mothers are back on the job shortly after their child is born. The child is either placed in a day-care facility, or cared for at home by hired help or in the home of a baby-sitter. Toddlers in diapers are put into programs or nursery schools that may be six to eight hours long. Many parents admit they still struggle with this decision and feel the sting of daily separation, which causes some tension and upheaval for both parent and child. Some parents continue to juggle their schedules while vacillating between having a career and being a stay-at-home mom or dad. In the past, a child's first day of school, at age five or six, caused some trauma of separation from the security of the home and family. Today, children at a very early age are expected to adjust to the new environment, new adults, new companions, and to acquire the skills they need to make this transition. Some kids do have amazing ability to adjust very readily to this schedule, while some continue to be affected and distressed by the separation. Another change in lifestyles is the fact that both parents are working longer hours, or, in the case of single parents, the job may be infringing on the needed supervision of and quality time with their kids.

New-Age Media

We already mentioned TV as a built-in baby-sitter, a vehicle for education, and an exploiter of violence, depicting different values and morals. Now we must add the age of computers, video games, music videos, and the Internet, which bring with them new challenges, more pressure, and more distress. Children must be cautioned about their involvement with on-line "chat rooms," pods, games, and Internet correspondence. Several cases have been documented where kids have been abducted or molested by someone they met through these on-line chat rooms. Some of the unsupervised materials and information can upset the kids and elicit a multitude of feelings and emotions the children are not yet ready to handle. Yet, we all know that the "Net" is here to stay; its possibilities are endless and unimagined. Kids can visit home pages and numerous historical, educational, and cultural sites. Many of these sites are interactive with music, art, and up-to-the-minute world news and personal e-mail messages. Computers are standard equipment in some schools, even though their value is questioned by certain educators. More and more younger children are proficient at their use. Kids have to be warned that there are some dangers out there. They should be encouraged to use common sense and to not take unnecessary chances.

Music

Music, rock groups, and lyrics have been known to have an effect on kids. The debate continues on whether this form of entertainment is responsible for the immoral and negative, sometimes destructive, behavior of some kids. If a child is already vulnerable, hearing a favorite singer or "rapper" constantly repeat a message to kill, hurt, or maim ourselves or somebody else could become a driving force, even a viable idea for some kids. Some evidence points to this reality when kids commit violent crimes and quote these messages as responsible for their choices. Since there are usually two sides to a story, we should also consider the very strong influence of Christian rock groups. They are growing in popularity, and they do have a significant positive effect on youth because they deliver a very moral message. What types of music do our children enjoy?

Movies

We have already mentioned the effect TV and videos can have in our kids' world. Modern movies deserve special mention at this time. Even with the rating system that movie studios use to police their industry, not many pictures are suitable for families. Many are violent, filled with sick individuals, with bizarre mutilating and murderous behavior, and scary, frightful pictures of creatures or aliens stalking and eating their victims. Even the coming attractions can impart the horror we will experience if we choose to see such-and-such film. When we go to the movies, what images do we like to see? What films do we patronize, and are they filled with our values and beliefs? As adults we can evaluate and scrutinize what is unfolding on the big screen. Can we use these films to educate our children and talk about the things they see, the messages and values or lack of values they learn from a film? Children cannot grow up in a protective bubble shielded from the influence of society; but they can be taught to evaluate, discern, and to make good moral judgments distinguishing good from evil, right from wrong, and reality from fantasy. Movies are supposed to be for entertainment, but they can also be used as a teaching tool.

Status

Most people seek status in one form or another. For adults and children, status means different things. Many adults find status in their community position, which means nothing to most kids. Children, especially older ones, find status in the clothes they wear or by "hanging out" with kids that others consider "cool." These dress codes are discussed later in this section.

Most well-meaning parents want the very best for their children. There are times when parents go overboard in giving their child an overabundance of things or privileges. There are also times when "parental pride" may exert an enormous amount of pressure, wanting the child to excel, *be* the "best," in the "best" school, or be the "best" player. This is more pressure than most children can handle. All children long for their basic needs to be met. They want to love and be loved. They want their parents to be there for them. Kids want to feel safe and secure; they want to feel constant and unconditional love from their parents, even if they mess up or misbehave. It is at those very times when kids seem to act unlovable or push us to our limit that they really need that physical hug or outward expression of love. Adults should try and convey to the children that they are not bad boys or bad girls, but, rather, that their actions or their behaviors were naughty, were a bad choice or unacceptable. Whenever we have the opportunity, we should try to sneak in some extra attention, hugs, or praise when the child least expects it and is not acting out. This works, and it can be very reassuring for the kids.

In other cases, the parental search for status for their kids extends to sports activities. Children should be encouraged to play sports, but sometimes even very tiny tots are being pushed too hard, too fast, by their parents and coaches so they will excel. Winning becomes the major goal, rather than playing the game for fun. This can be most distressful, especially for the child who is trying to please the parent but really does not have the desire to play or the athletic ability. A six-year-old told his friend that his dad was a great football player. He said, "I really hate football, but my dad likes me when I play, so I have to play." If kids are not forced to play, sports are an excellent arena to emphasize fun, self-improvement, resiliency, to learn self-control, and a way to encourage kids to be cooperative, even sometimes noncompetitive.

Other children are "strongly encouraged" to take music or dance lessons. Again, if this is not their choice, it will add tremendous amounts of unnecessary distress. A seven-year-old told me, "Mommy wants me to be a ballerina because her best friend's kid is one. I hate it, so I keep falling down and wishing I could break my leg so she'd let me out of it." Other children have developed psychosomatic ailments, ranging from stomach pain, nausea, or vomiting, to dizziness and headaches, in order to get out of the "game" or music/dance lesson. Do our children want to be ballerinas or athletes? If so, then we can encourage them to have fun and feel good about their improvement and their successes. They will thank us later for the wonderful opportunities we provided them.

Dress Code

Another source of distress comes from the societal "dress code." Children who cannot afford name-brand clothing or $125 sneakers are embarrassed or ashamed or mocked by their peers. This adds to their low self-esteem, which then sets them up to be vulnerable. They need to know that "clothes do not make the person." This statement may seem passé or totally outdated, especially when we see the clothes, costumes, and outfits of rock groups and TV stars. Are these clothes we would want to wear?

What message do they send? Are these acceptable outfits for our kids? This is where children can learn about diversity and individuality. Despite their cry for independence and "I've got to be me," they feel they do not belong unless they wear a certain fad clothing, or have orange hair, or wear an earring or two or eight in every orifice or pierceable part of their anatomy. Obviously, kids want to fit in. They want to have friends, and at certain ages they believe the only way to do this is to dress like the others. Self-esteem, self-confidence, and security play a strong role in the dress codes children establish among themselves. Parental support and limits also come into play. These are not really criticisms or judgments, just observations. We all know some very good, solid, wonderful kids who choose to follow the common dress code as they go through a phase or try to make an outrageous statement. We also know other kids who follow their family values and Christian way of life, and choose not to dress in that way. Strong family support, faith in God, and moral values can help kids combat some of the societal influences they face.

Gangs

Gangs can strongly affect kids and society. They are a powerful presence, not only in our big cities, but also in the suburbs. Gangs can look very inviting to fragile kids. The most vulnerable ones may try experimenting with drugs, sex, or belonging to the gang in order to "fit in." Gangs have very clear-cut rules, limits, and guidelines. If kids do not find those limits at home, enforced by their parents, or if they feel they are not valued or listened to, they seek support elsewhere.

We must listen to our kids, love them, let them know they belong with us and our family. We'll set limits and let our kids know they will be enforced, even if the kids challenge them and push us to the limits. We must not give up on them. They need us, our love, support, boundaries, and rules.

Here are some stories the kids told me about what they did because they were looking for a way to fit in and feel loved.

Fourteen-year-old Lisa said, "I needed to be with my friends so I tried sex, and I got pregnant. My mom wanted me to get an abortion and I said no. At least now I have somebody to love and take care of."

A twelve-year-old boy robbed two little old ladies coming home from the store. "I had to get my sneakers so the kids didn't think I was a geek. I needed to get over $100 'cause my dad wouldn't give me more money."

Thirteen-year-old Sara started to hang out on the corner with kids she really didn't like. She started to feel accepted, started smoking pot, and slowly graduated to stronger, more dangerous drugs.

111

Some kids will steal after they experience a major loss such as the death of a loved one or parental divorce, or just to try to fit in. They have deep feelings of deprivation, so to fill that void and feel better, they resort to stealing or some other destructive behavior.

These societal pressure stories could go on and on. Each of these children was distressed and would try anything to be a part of the group. In the absence of authority figures and good role models, more children will succumb to peer pressures and alternative forms of behavior. If children are not taught appropriate stress responses and given tools to deal with these issues, they can become hopeless and depressed, which could lead to a gamut of self-destructive behaviors and many more kids in crisis.

Poverty

According to the 1997 research report, *Kids Count Data Book–State Profiles of Child Well-Being,* from the Annie E. Casey Foundation in Baltimore, Maryland, about 7 million children are growing up in poor communities. Researchers found that a greater number of these kids are at risk of being sick, being parents themselves before they graduate, and being drug users. They are exposed to violence and may wind up in jail before they are legally able to vote. The report continues by saying that some kids and families from these poor neighborhoods will be strong, resilient, and rise above the debilitating environment, but some of the other kids will grow up and not be prepared to be a parent, work, or contribute to society.

This research paints a sad picture for some of our youth. They need our help, guidance, and support. Many kids are searching for their values, morals, and individual ways to cope with all this. Some of them do have hope, and many are relying on their faith and church community to find the answers so they can live good, happy, productive lives. How are we going to help them with their world and enable them to reach their goals? The answer keeps coming up that parents, teachers, and mentors must strive to give kids unconditional love, acceptance, respect, and support.

7

WHAT CAN PARENTS AND TEACHERS DO?

An Awesome Responsibility

Teachers and parents have an absolutely awesome responsibility. They have one of the most challenging, and yet most rewarding, professions. As difficult as some of the kids are, that classroom or that home must still be filled with love, laughter, and learning. It is the backbone of future generations. We know kids can't be perfect, but most do want to learn. They feel so good about themselves whenever they pass a test or finish a project, clean their room, or learn and understand a new concept. They feel wonderful when they see that we are also pleased by their success. Kids learn very early in life to try to please their parents and teachers, and believe this will get them the love and care they need. It is a good idea to help kids assess their own work and teach them to look within for their own approval. We can teach them to assess their own performance rather than to look for praise and approval from outsiders. This can help protect kids from peer pressure, from doing something wrong just to be accepted.

Sharing Family Time

For the sake of the generations to come, we must continue to nurture the family, making it grow strong and healthy. To do this, some families set aside quality time to share and communicate, to build up positive and beautiful memories for the future. Some set aside one night a week as a time for a family meeting where they catch up with each other, plan, and share. Other families plan very special outings or take weekend trips whenever possible. Many families make it a priority to celebrate, in a very special way, any occasion when they can be together— birthdays, anniversaries, promotions, graduations, religious milestones, and other rites of passage. In these times together, families learn how to give and receive love, share their values, their faith and beliefs, and learn interpersonal skills of mutual caring and respect for one another. In family celebrations, ethnic and cultural values are passed on to the next generation. Within this nurturing atmosphere, children feel secure, loved, and encouraged to become self-confident and caring adults who, in turn, will raise their children in the same manner. If each generation could instill and practice this mutual caring and respect for one another, it could help eliminate some of the selfishness and violence in our society.

Seeking Accurate Diagnoses

One special area for parents, teachers, and caregivers to investigate is the tremendous number of children being diagnosed with attention deficit disorders. Experts have now discovered that a large number of these children may have other problems, such as depression or learning disabilities. An accurate diagnosis is needed so that the affected children receive the appropriate help. Some children have been diagnosed with hyperactive and behavior problems, but after further tests their physicians discovered they had food allergies.

Parents are cautioned to seek an accurate diagnosis for their child. If the child has a behavioral problem, classification under the umbrella of attention deficit should not be used as a convenience or easy solution. This does not benefit either party. Every avenue should be explored so the child can feel better about him/herself and be enabled to experience success and decreased frustration.

Building (Blocks) To Self-Esteem

The process of establishing self-esteem can begin when a baby is first playing with blocks. Parents must observe their kids and watch for either success or possible frustration. They must refrain from doing the task for the children. Otherwise, they will not be able to discover their own power, learn from their mistakes, and experience the thrill of success. We can tell if our kids are getting overwhelmed or too distressed as they try to complete a task. If they are frustrated we can show them, encourage them, or do it together. There must be a balance between praise and criticism. Too much of either is not beneficial to children. Too much praise leads to seeking approval from others without personal satisfaction; too much criticism teaches kids how to be critical of others and creates feelings of despair and hopelessness. When they are faced with new tasks and challenges in school or in life, they may feel frustrated, inadequate, and give up. We are not always going to be there to help them or do it for them. Allowing them to experience success and some failure helps them prepare for the real world and teaches them some problem-solving skills. To help them gauge their progress, we can ask them the following questions:

☆ ☆ ☆

"How did you feel when you did that?"

"Are you pleased with the mark you received on your paper?"

"Was this your best work?"

"Do you believe you could have done any better?"

"Did you try/study as hard as you could?"

"Did you do your best in cleaning your room (or whatever project was completed)?"

☆ ☆ ☆

A kid's first response will probably be, "Yeah, sure, it's my best effort." Eventually, when children are asked to look within and answer honestly, they will experience some personal satisfaction. They will not have to depend on others for their measure of success or approval. They can pat themselves on the shoulder and say "good for me, good job, I did it. It was my very best and I am really pleased." If they can learn to do this, they will not grow up looking to outsiders for their love, approval, and support. Some adults are still searching for this validation from others for their accomplishments. When they do not receive it, they feel unsuccessful and filled with self-doubt, believing they are "not good enough or did not do a wonderful job." Some praise is good for our children, but by helping them to assess their performance honestly, not judging it falsely or harshly, we ensure that they learn another important lesson in developing a healthy self-esteem. This is a lifelong process which began in the home and continues to be nurtured at school. As kids continue to know, love, and approve of themselves, they will acknowledge their gifts and strive to reach their God-given potential.

Stress-Busters

We have read about the home, school, and society as major areas of distress in the life of kids. Throughout this book, ideas were mentioned and certain suggestions were made to help us and the kids in different situations. The following sections provide suggestions for specific stress-busters.

We know that human beings consist of body, mind, spirit, and emotions, so we will discuss these specific techniques under the categories of physical, spiritual, and mental relaxation. We can practice these stress-relievers and then adapt them to the age-appropriate level for our children.

Physical Relaxation Reduces Stress In Our Bodies

☆ ☆ ☆

(NOTE: Any physical activity should be done only on the advice and approval of your physician.)

☆ ☆ ☆

When we are distressed, it is recommended that we do something physical. When we are physically exhausted, we need to let our body rest. The wisdom is in knowing the difference.

Walking is a proven stress-reliever that not only helps our bodies but also clears our minds or enlightens our thoughts. If physically able, we should try to take a scheduled walk, park our car at the far end of a parking lot rather than near the door, or climb a set or two of stairs instead of using the elevator. There are a variety of physical activities that will suit our individual needs and level of distress. Here is a random list: ride a bicycle; do the treadmill; play racquetball, volleyball, paddleball, or any other sport. Swim; jump rope; run; punch a punching bag or shadow box. Dance to some favorite '50s records or fast music; jazzercise; run in place; do jumping jacks, toe-touches, or sit-ups; use hand weights (a can of soup in each hand can substitute) or strength-building machines. Fitness experts state that we should exercise at least 20 minutes a day in an activity that will safely raise our pulse rate. Undoubtedly, this will help lessen our distress. Another common physical technique is to sit down and relax the whole body. Starting with our toes, we can progressively begin to tighten and release the muscles throughout our body.

We all have heard of the right and left brain function. There is another physical movement which can revive us, help alleviate stress, enhance our creativity, and help us to feel alert and energized. Any time we have been in meetings or concentrating intensely for a long while, we could try this exercise. Stand and raise the right arm and left foot as if marching, then continue by raising the left arm and right foot; alternate sides and continue marching in place for at least a few minutes. This movement, according to experts in right and left brain studies, is supposed to balance both hemispheres of the brain so we are not straining one side over the other. As the balance occurs, we feel mentally alert and ready to begin again. Given some practice and patience, we will be pleasantly surprised that it can and does work.

Spiritual Relaxation

The best path to spiritual relaxation is to be still. In Scripture we are told "Be still and know that I am God" (Psalm 46:11). Prayer, contemplation, and meditation lead us inward to relax and renew our relationship with God. In silence we can just listen and be aware of the God spirit within us. There are a variety of ways we can use to reach that peaceful state of serenity and calm. We might use soft music, take deep breaths, and slowly count down from ten to zero as we deliberately inhale and exhale. We can use whatever really works to help us slow down and begin to relax. One relaxing form of meditation is simply to pray the name of Jesus. We sit quietly, with our eyes closed. As we inhale deeply, we mentally say the first syllable "JE," hold for a second or two; then exhale slowly and mentally say "SUS." We can repeat this prayer often to calm our breathing and keep away distracting thoughts.

When we review the life of Jesus, we read about the things he did most often. He went up to the mountain either alone or with his friends, he went to the beach and seashore often, and he frequently ate at the homes of others. He took the time and space he needed to relax, fill his cup, and deepen his relationship with the Father. He also shared, ate, laughed, and prayed with his friends and strengthened those relationships. Jesus was truly the example, and we should live, learn, and do likewise.

We can make a place of solitude for meditation and relaxation anywhere we want. Some people set aside a corner of their room and make this their sacred space. One beautiful meditation is to picture ourselves in a favorite place of relaxation. It is recommended that this be a place in nature, on the beach, in the mountains, under the shade of a beautiful tree. Here is a description of my favorite place: It is near the ocean, and I am walking on the beach heading for a safe cave in the side of the hill. I enter the cave and immediately I am in a wide-open space with a little pond surrounded by rocks and flowers. The sunlight is streaming down, yet there is a pleasant, cooling breeze. The sky is a beautiful blue interspersed with fluffs of white clouds. I sit on the side of the pond, lean comfortably against a rock, and place my feet in the cool, soothing water. I breathe deeply and just enjoy the sound of the ocean and the smell of the flowers. There are times I just sit there, just relax and free my mind of any thoughts. Other times I picture Jesus sitting on the rocks with me. I talk to Jesus in my mind, sharing what is going on in my life. I thank God for my gifts and blessings, ask for guidance in a particular situation, or simply pray for others. This is the place where I renew and refresh my spirit, feed my soul, and fill my spiritual cup. We can create our own safe, sacred space where we can commune with God, be filled with the Holy Spirit, and be free of tension, worry, fear, or anxiety.

Another truly great medicine for the soul is the gift of humor. Our sense of humor is deeply rooted in our spirituality. Humor and laughter have been said to physically activate our immune system to help restore our inner balance. Each person has that mischievous, loving, joyful little child within us no matter what our age. Humor helps us to release that playful child who, over the years of growth and maturity, we have learned to stifle and keep hidden within us. Now is the time we should free that little child and give him/her permission to laugh and play a little bit more each day. We have all heard that life is too short. Adding a little more laughter and play in our lives will not lead to irresponsibility. The ability to laugh at ourselves and not take ourselves so seriously is a wonderful distress reliever, one we should always nurture. Being able to laugh at our minor mistakes or mishaps helps to lighten our spirit, so we don't respond with intense anger or undue disgust at what we did. It is common knowledge that it takes more facial muscles (and a serious waste of energy) to frown rather than smile. Jesus reminds us that he came to give us abundant life and that we are meant to savor the joy of that life. Our ultimate goal and challenge in life is to maintain balance and integrate our body, mind, spirit, and emotions. It is up to us to encourage joy, laughter, and that integration of who we are in the children we meet.

Mental Relaxation

We talk to ourselves all day long. That chatter or self-talk is going to build us up or tear us down. In these mental conversations, we will either use positive affirmations to build up our self-confidence, or negative comments to clutter our minds with fear, worry, and anxiety. Instead of a typical coffee break, we can give ourselves a mental-health break. It will truly be for our well-being and better health to take these soothing, refreshing, mental periods of time and space. In the middle of a tumultuous day, and within a matter of seconds, we can picture ourselves relaxing on the beach in Hawaii, without leaving our swivel chair. We can imagine ourselves in our favorite place of relaxation wherever that may be. It is in this place that we mentally repeat an affirmation, visualize our goals, a presentation, or tasks we wish to complete. We picture these, taking them to a successful completion. We can take a few deep breaths and imagine ourselves being filled with peace, love, and energy. This is similar to the "60-second stress-reliever." It is something each one of us has the power to do, and only the individual can do it. As soon as we feel our minds on overload, or feel that we are not concentrating, it's time to take this mental-health break. We can also use this time to picture our loved ones having a wonderful, distress-free day. It is during these periods that we can pray and just spend our time relaxed in the Lord. These mental breaks refill and renew our strength and enable us to be rejuvenated. A mother can put her baby down for a nap, or say to a little one that Mommy needs a time-out and invite the child to sit quietly with her. We can teach our children to use this mental break to help themselves slow down, pray, visualize their goals or successful game, or to just relax and fill their cup with love and peace.

Another technique that can help us to eliminate some worry or anxiety, especially if our mind is racing and creating scary thoughts, is to mentally relax and hold an absorbing picture in our mind. For example, let's say we love sunflowers. Well, first we sit quietly and take a few deep breaths. Then we visualize one big beautiful sunflower, and then a few more of them. We keep enhancing our picture until we see nothing but rows and rows of beautiful, bright, yellow sunflowers with their big brown centers stretching as far as our eye can see. If we are picturing the flowers, we cannot be thinking of the fear or worry. We can only think one thought at a time.

The secret of relaxation techniques is to give ourselves permission to do them. Only we can make the choice, take and set aside the time to make them happen. We are so programmed to go, do, and be busy, sometimes we feel guilty because we believe we are being lazy or unproductive. We owe it to ourselves; it is a form of the theology of self-care. Theology means "of God" and we all have a mandate to love our neighbor as ourselves. Part of that love must be self-care. We are not talking about selfishness or self-absorption. If we do not take care of ourselves and our mental, physical, and spiritual health, no one else can or will do that for us. I saw a postcard recently with these words of wisdom by Kobi Yamada: "Be good to yourself. Take care of yourself. Take care of your body. If you don't, where will you live?" We need to take good care of ourselves so we can be there to model this loving behavior for our children. They will see that we love ourselves, and them, enough to take care of and make smart choices for our better health. We teach our kids by word and lived example that they can make good choices to reduce their daily distress and learn to take care of themselves, so they can live and love in a happier, healthier home and society.

8

Bloom and Grow
to the Fullest

Our Most Treasured Gifts

Home and school are still the most valuable and essential institutions in our society. Children are still our most valuable and treasured gifts. Parents have the awesome privilege to plant the seeds of love, truth, faith, and trust in their children. They have the responsibility to be role models and to nurture their kids' self-esteem and moral development. They have the incomparable power to water them with love, affection, support, and the encouragement they need. They provide limits and the guidance kids need so they can blossom into strong, healthy, happy, mature,

responsible adults. Louise Hay, author and metaphysical counselor, in her book *You Can Heal Your Life*, tells the story of a tomato seed. We plant the seed, nurture it with sunshine, water, and love. This tomato plant has the potential to grow big and tall and bear hundreds of tomatoes. When the little plant sticks its head above the ground and begins to get bigger, do we stomp on it and say, "Where are all the tomatoes?" No, we continue the process of love, water, sunshine, and nurturing so it can reach its full potential. How true is this story for all of us and for the kids. We are not done yet. We are all still in process, trying to grow to the fullest, reach our potential, and be the person God has called us to be. As children enter their school years, teachers and caregivers sustain this nurturing process as they encourage kids to face new challenges and to handle the distress they face each day. From the safety, love, and security of the family and school, kids can go forth better equipped with the tools they need as they branch out into society. Kids will mirror the adults in their lives. Will that image reflect people with strong values and morals, filled with acceptance, tolerance, and unconditional love for themselves and others? Will that image reflect future generations filled with empathy, respect for human life, care for the property of others, and serve as faithful custodians of the planet? The kids today will be the adults of tomorrow. Are we giving them the tools and skills they need for a better life? Will their kids grow up in a peace-filled, less violent society, or will their kids be distressed, too? We must love and cherish our children, for they are irreplaceable treasures and gifts from God.